MEXICAN WRITERS
on Writing

Whatever their excellence and variety, Mexican authors for centuries lived and wrote nearly unknown to a North American public. Now, in a collection spanning the full range of the country's history, celebrated translator Margaret Sayers Peden gathers a rich array of writings to bring Mexico's literature to light.

From the literature of colonialism and conquest to a contemporary look at Mexican life and letters, these writers reveal ever-changing views of what it is to be a writer and just how flexible the boundaries of what we have termed "literature" can be.

CONTRIBUTORS

Bernardo de Balbuena
Carmen Boullosa
Emilio Carballido
Ricardo Chávez Castañeda
Rosario Castellanos
Sor Juana Inés de la Cruz
Bartolomé de las Casas
José Joaquín Fernández
   de Lizardi
Carlos Fuentes
Margo Glantz
Enrique González Martínez

Angeles Mastretta
José Emilio Pacheco
Ignacio Padilla
Pedro Ángel Palou
Octavio Paz
Elena Poniatowska
Alberto Ruy Sánchez
Ilan Stavans
Eloy Urroz
Juan Villoro
Jorge Volpi

THE WRITER'S WORLD
Edward Hirsch, SERIES EDITOR

The Writer's World features writers from around the globe discussing what it means to write, and to be a writer, in many different parts of the world. The series collects a broad range of material and provides access for the first time to a body of work never before gathered in English. Edward Hirsch, the series editor, is internationally acclaimed as a poet and critic. He is the president of the John Simon Guggenheim Foundation.

Irish Writers on Writing
EDITED BY Eavan Boland

Mexican Writers on Writing
EDITED BY Margaret Sayers Peden

Polish Writers on Writing
EDITED BY Adam Zagajewski

Trinity University Press gratefully acknowledges the generous support of the following Patrons of The Writer's World:

Sarah Harte and John Gutzler
Mach Family Fund, Joella and Steve Mach

MEXICAN WRITERS

on Writing

EDITED BY

Margaret Sayers Peden

TRINITY UNIVERSITY PRESS
San Antonio, Texas

Published by Trinity University Press
San Antonio, Texas 78212

Cover design by Karen Schober
Book design by BookMatters, Berkeley

⊗ The paper used in this publication meets the minimum requirements
of the American National Standard for Information Sciences—
Permanence of Paper for Printed Library Materials, ANSI Z39.48-1992.

Printed on 100% post-consumer waste recycled text stock.

Library of Congress Cataloging-in-Publication Data
 Mexican writers on writing / edited by Margaret Sayers Peden.
    p.   cm. —(The writer's world)
  SUMMARY: "Ranging from the literature of colonialism and
  conquest to a contemporary look at Mexican life and letters, the
  book presents a cross-section of Mexican authors' thoughts on
  writing, including works by Carlos Fuentes, Bernardo de
  Balbuena, Sor Juana Inés de la Cruz, Octavio Paz, Elena
  Poniatowska, and others."—PROVIDED BY PUBLISHER.
 Includes bibliographical references and index.
   ISBN-13: 978-1-59534-028-3 (hardcover : alk. paper)
   ISBN-10: 1-59534-028-9 (hardcover : alk. paper)
   ISBN-13: 978-1-59534-034-4 (pbk. : alk. paper)
   ISBN-10: 1-59534-034-3 (pbk. : alk. paper)
  1. Mexican literature.   2. Authors, Mexican-Literary collections.
  I. Peden, Margaret Sayers.
 PQ7236.5.A98M49   2007
 860.9'972—dc22   2006037076

11   10   09   08   07   C   5   4   3   2   1

Contents

Preface

Margaret Sayers Peden

Language creates a difficult barrier, one that the visual, musical, and plastic arts can span, but Mexico's long history of letters, beginning with the reports and chronicles of the first conquistadors and missionaries, remains largely unknown to us. We have no full knowledge of the oral tradition the Spanish found upon their arrival in the early 1500s, though the fragments that survived, among them poems and a story of creation, hint at a rich and beautiful tradition. Neither the Aztecs nor the Maya — in fact, no pre-Columbian Indian tribe — had a written language, and nearly all of their painted codices were destroyed by Catholic priests who had been sent to Christianize the New World.

The sixteenth century — those early years of discovery, exploration, and subduing indigenous peoples in order to impose the European culture of the conquistadors — abounds in chronicles and letters. While these writings were not intended as literature, they are, nonetheless, a fascinating body of materials in which their authors report, not infrequently with exaggeration, their own feats, along with the wondrous landscapes and cities and peoples they encounter. They also debate among themselves, and with authorities in Spain, the spiritual and cultural state of the peoples they had been sent to convert to Spain's religious and social customs, questions such as whether the Indians did indeed have souls. Among the many missionary priests whose philosophies and opinions have been left to us, we might mention especially Fray Bartolomé de las Casas, Fray Andrés de Olmos, Fray Bernardino de Sahagún, and Fray Juan Suárez de Peralta. Of the conquista-

dors, two are of particular interest because of the written records they left of
the historic encounter between the Old and the New Worlds. The first is
Hernán Cortés, the conqueror of Mexico and nemesis of Moctezuma. In
five letters known as the *Cartas de Relación*, he naively depicts the cruelty of
the Spaniards as well as the grandeur of Mexico that Bernardo de Balbuena
would glorify in his epic poem. The second conquistador of note is one of
Cortés's soldiers, Bernal Díaz de Castillo, whose *Verdadera historia de la con-
quista de Nueva España* (True History of the Conquest of New Spain), is perhaps the most minutely detailed account of the day-to-day activities of the
encounter.

Because of the difficulties of communication, the first priests found that
theater was an efficient medium for teaching, and they wrote, or adapted,
works they used as visual illustrations of the sacraments and the practices of
the church. Poetry, a genre deeply ingrained in Mexican culture, reached its
highest expression in that period in Balbuena's epic *Grandeza de Mexico*, and
though his novel, *El siglo de oro en las junglas de Erífile* (The Golden Age in the
Jungles of Erífile, 1608), can be considered a pastoral work, one might have
expected that in a culture that produced the Quijote in 1605, it would not
take two more centuries before a more conventional novel was written in
Mexico.

Considering the large numbers of chroniclers, there were relatively few
novelists and playwrights and poets. We must speculate that they were busy
subduing and converting the indigenous peoples, searching for El Dorado,
founding cities, building churches, dwellings, and schools — in short, establishing Spain's presence. The men who responded to the lure of glory and
wealth were men of action, not artists or intellectuals, and they were immediately plunged into life-endangering adventures, which did not leave much
time for the literary life.

The end of the sixteenth and first half of the seventeenth centuries
in Mother Spain saw one of the world's greatest flowering of writers:
Garcilaso, Lope de Vega, Góngora, Quevedo, Cervantes, Calderón, Tirso
de Molina. . . . The list goes on. It was, as we know, the Golden Age of
Spain, a glorious age for the arts. And in seventeenth-century Mexico a
writer of equal stature emerged, a truly monumental figure: Sor Juana Inés
de la Cruz. By this time, Mexico City was a sophisticated city with a vicere-

gal court, theaters, universities, salons, fine gowns, and elegant receptions for visiting nobility. Sor Juana had the mixed blessing of being born at a time when intellect and literary talents were revered but also a time when brilliance was not expected in a woman. The seventeenth century also produced Juan Ruiz de Alarcón, a Mexican-born playwright who is included among Spain's famous Golden Age dramatists, and a friend and colleague of Sor Juana, a monk with a similarly searching mind, Carlos de Sigüenza y Góngora.

The Baroque and the Rococo of the early eighteenth century find little resonance with contemporary literary tastes, and those modes quickly faded in Mexico as well. Later in the century, some of the stormy winds and ideas circulating through Europe, the thunder of the French and North American revolutions, rumbled across Mexico. The beginnings of a movement for independence can be found in the writings of Fray Servando Teresa de Mier, who lived some years in Europe, and who was an early advocate of Mexican emancipation. His memories and various writings protest his treatment as an American, that is, as a person inferior to his counterparts in Spain.

For three centuries, from the time of the Encounter up to the nineteenth century, Mexico's influences had been homogeneous; everything from language, to religion, to architecture, to governmental structure, to literature had come by way of Spain, but now a century of political turmoil and wars would change those patterns. The struggle for independence from Spain began with the Grito en Dolores in 1810. In 1821 Spain accepted Mexico's independence, but that led not to a period of peace but to a chaotic series of wars: the Texas revolution in 1836; war with the French in 1838; with the United States, 1846–48 (when Mexico lost New Mexico and California); internal conflicts over reform, 1858–61; and another French intervention with the brief reign of Maximilian, 1864–67. Finally in 1867, Maximilian was executed and Benito Juárez started his second term as president of Mexico. There was, nevertheless, still another dictatorship to be survived: that of Porfirio Díaz, begun in 1876 and ended in 1910 with the outbreak of the Mexican Revolution.

Despite this great period of social instability, literary influences broadened. Mexican writers turned toward Europe, and they adopted, with slight delays, the literary movements of that century: romanticism and naturalism in the novel, along with the Parnassian and symbolist schools in poetry. Around 1888, Latin American writers made their own contribution to the list of literary modes, *modernismo*. This movement — not to be confused with late-twentieth-century Modernism — espoused art for art's sake and was at times dangerously prone to *preciosité*, though it produced some excellent poets in Central America and the Southern Cone.

It was at the height of *modernismo* that any conformity in literary modes was forever ended, for just as its dominance began to wane, *Los de abajo* (The Underdogs) by Mariano Azuela was published, a robust work depicting the revolutionary war against class and church. It would be difficult to imagine a greater contrast than that between the swans and princesses of *modernismo* and the populist heroes of the Novel of the Revolution.

It seems inevitable that future scholars and historians will define the twentieth century as Mexico's Golden Age. The poems of Enrique González Martínez, who had himself followed the tenets of the *modernista* movement only to contribute to its demise, the experimental poetry of short-lived clamor of the *estridentistas*, the classic calm of an essayist philosopher named Alfonso Reyes, and the many works of an avant-garde group of young writers called the Contemporáneos, who had eyes only for Europe and who formed one of the most cohesive groups in Mexican letters, all coexisted with continuing examples of the Novel of the Revolution and the sensual, innovative poetry of Ramón López Velarde.

Three giants stand out in the multicolored tapestry of the twentieth century: the Nobel laureate Octavio Paz, the brilliant novelist Carlos Fuentes, and a quiet, melancholy man named Juan Rulfo, a cult figure in Mexico who wrote only a collection of short stories and a novel entitled *Pedro Páramo* — but who nonetheless is lionized by generations of Latin American writers.

Whatever their excellence and variety, Mexican authors for centuries lived and wrote nearly unknown to a North American public. Two transformative events opened literary channels across the Rio Grande — the Second World War and the literary phenomenon known as The Boom. Several things happened during and after the war. Given the difficulties of communication with Europe — specifically Spain and France — Mexican artists turned inward, toward this hemisphere. The Spanish Civil War that had preceded the Second World War also had brought an influx of exiled intellectuals to Mexico that enriched Mexico's artistic communities. And a Mexican publishing industry developed that broke a long dependence on Spanish publishing houses.

Even with the internal changes wrought during the 1940s and 1950s, it would not be until the 1960s, and the explosion of The Boom, that Mexican — indeed Latin American — writers would begin to emerge onto the international scene. The Argentine Jorge Luis Borges was the forerunner of this new recognition. North American readers discovered Borges not directly, but through the French, who awarded him the Formentor prize in 1961. What followed was a true flood of critically acclaimed writers. Gabriel García Márquez, Julio Cortázar, Carlos Fuentes, and Mario Vargas Llosa were the first to have their novels translated and published in the United States, soon followed by many others, mostly novelists, among them José Donoso, Ernesto Sábato, Alejo Carpentier, Miguel Angel Asturias, Juan Carlos Onetti, Guillermo Cabrera Infante, José Lezama Lima, Eduardo Mallea, Jorge Edwards, and the Mexicans Juan Rulfo, Salvador Elizondo, Gustavo Sainz, Fernando del Paso, Luis Arturo Ramos, the playwright Emilio Carballido, and in poetry José Emilio Pacheco (also a novelist), and of course Paz.

This is an impressive list, and the combined talents of these Latin American authors are formidable. But in that gathering, there is one enormous lacuna: there is not a single woman writer. Women weren't writing? They were, of course. It would take another twenty years, however, for women to make the same breakthrough that male writers had already achieved. And like male writers, once the floodgates opened, their talent began to flow outward in English translation. The Chilean writer Isabel Allende has a following that parallels that of major male writers, and Mexico's Margo Glantz, Rosario Castellanos, Silvia Molina, Elena Poniatowska, Elena Garro, Carmen Boullosa, Alma Guillermoprieto, Laura Esquivel, and Angeles Mastretta all signal the dawn of a new era.

The emphasis here on works that appeared in English translation is intended only as an indicator of North American awareness of the wealth of writers south of our border, writers we had not acknowledged because we were unaware of their existence. There are many excellent authors who will continue to produce fine literature that does not need English language translation as imprimatur. In turn, North American literature is speedily translated into Spanish and sales often supercede those of Mexico's own authors. A great deal of this must be laid at the feet of marketing and publicity, which often have little to do with literary values. But what is important is that there *are* openings in the cactus curtain, a measure of free literary exchange, and it may be that one day a natural balance will be achieved.

But to the point of Mexican writers on writing. The pieces collected here present a cross section of Mexican authors' thoughts on writing, from Fuentes's instructional decalogue, to Balbuena's flowery dissertation on the beauty of poetry, to Paz's analysis of the essence of translation. From the Conquest to Crack (a twentieth-century movement referring to the sound of "rupture"), these writers reveal ever-changing views of what it is to be a writer and just how flexible the boundaries of what we have termed literature can be.

Bartolomé de las Casas

(1484 – 1566)

An Account, Much Abbreviated, of the Destruction of the Indies

It would be a stretch to identify Bartolomé de las Casas as Mexican. There was no "Mexico" at the time he was writing. Las Casas was Spanish, a priest, and a historian. He was also a humanist and a ferocious defender of the New World's indigenous peoples, the first to speak out on their behalf for social and political justice.

Las Casas was present at Columbus's triumphant return to Seville in 1493, and he himself traveled many times between the Old and New Worlds, often to plead the cause of the Indians to his king, Emperor Charles V. He also attempted to enact laws to protect the conquered indigenous peoples from slavery and genocide, and to promote his Utopian view of the New World and its inhabitants.

One of the worst institutions initiated by the Spanish was the *encomienda*, a practice in which the conquistadors and colonists were granted "ownership" of the inhabitants of conquered land. However, in his eagerness to argue the Indians' cause, Las Casas suggested a strange, socially blind resolution: to save Indians from mistreatment by the *encomenderos* and colonists, blacks should be brought from Africa to substitute for them—the beginnings of the slave trade in the Americas.

Bartolomé de las Casas enjoyed a long life, seventy-four years of which were lived during the conquest and colonization of vast unexplored lands. He was the first priest ordained in the New World and was invested as the first bishop of Chiapas in 1544, then part of the "Kingdom of Guatemala" and now the southernmost state of Mexico.

Las Casas's words open this selection of Mexican writers on writing because they not only convey his frustration and horror at the treatment of the inhabitants of the New World but also reflect his compulsion to use *writing* as a weapon against oppression and injustice. *An Account, Much Abbreviated, of the Destruction of the Indies* is not a book about literary art and practice; it is a sociological study that for centuries has cast a dark shadow over the comportment of European conquerors in their encounter with unknown civilizations and peoples. In that sense, Las Casas is the grandfather of countless Mexican writers, the first in the long stream of Mexico's socio-political commentators, whether novelists, poets, dramatists, or essayists. Mexico has its fabulists and its romantics, but it is fair to say that more writing has been motivated by moral outrage like that of Bartolomé de las Casas than by any other imperative. His need to employ the written word to effect social change has echoed through generations of Mexican writers, from the author of the first Mexican novel, José Joaquín Fernández de Lizardi, to Carlos Fuentes, Mexico's best-known contemporary author.

The brief paragraphs that follow are from the opening pages of Las Casas's *Destruction of the Indies,* published in a new and complete translation by Andrew Hurley in 2003.

ARGUMENT OF THE PRESENT EPITOME

All the things that have taken place in the Indies, both since their marvelous discovery and those first years when Spaniards first went out to them to remain for some time, and then in the process thereafter down to these our own days, have been so extraordinary and so in no wise to be believed by any person who did not see them, that they seem to have clouded and laid silence and oblivion upon all those other deeds, however bold and dauntless they might be, that in centuries past were ever seen and heard in this world. Among these terrible things are the slaughters and ruins of people, the depopulations of villages, provinces, and kingdoms in those Indies, and many other acts of no less heinous and abominable character. Respecting these acts, the Bishop don Fray Bartolomé de las Casas or Casaus, after having been made a friar, came to Court to inform the Emperor our lord, who had ever looked with approval upon all these things. And Las Casas, chancing also to narrate these deeds to divers persons who did not know of them, caused a manner of ecstasy and suspension of spirit in his hearers with his narration, and he was begged and importuned to put some of them, briefly, into writing. And so he did, but seeing some years later many insensible men, brought by their covetousness and ambition to fall from the estate of humanity and led by their wicked deeds to reprobate mind (as the Bible sayeth), and not content with the treasons and mischief that they have committed, depopulating that realm with exquisite forms of cruelty, but yet importuning the king for license and authority to commit those acts yet again, and others yet worse (if worse there might be) — , that same Las Casas has determined to present this summary of our lord, so that His Highness might be led, by reading it, to refuse those petitions. And it has seemed to Las Casas meet that these things be printed so that His Highness might read them with greater ease. And that is the purpose of the following Epitome, or account, most highly abbreviated.

Presentation by Bishop don Fray Bartolomé de las Casas or Casaus, to the most high and potent lord Prince of all the Spains don Felipe, our lord

Most high and potent lord:

Because divine providence has ordered in this world that for the direction and common utility of the human lineage the world be constituted by Kingdoms and people, with their kings like fathers and shepherds (as Homer called them) and therefore the most noble and generous members of the republics, for that reason no doubt of the rectitude of the royal spirits of those kings may be held, or with right reason might be held. And if any wrongs, failings, defects, or evils should be suffered in those kingdoms, the only reason for that is that the kings have no notice of them. For these wrongs &c, if they be present and reported, it is the duty of the king, with greatest study and vigilant industry, to root them out. This appears to have been the meaning of divine scripture in the proverbs of Solomon: *Rex qui sedet in solio iudicii, dissipat omne malum intuito suo.* For it is clear that with the innate and natural virtue of the king, the mere notice of wrong or malefaction in his kingdom more than suffices for him to scatter it, and should such ills arise, not for a single moment could he tolerate them.

Considering, then, most potent lord, the evils and harm, the perditions and ruin — the equals or likes of which, never were men imagined capable of doing — considering, as I say, those evils which as a man of fifty years' and more experience, being in those lands present, I have seen committed upon those so many and such great kingdoms, or better said, that entire vast and new world of the Indies — lands conceded and given in trust by God and His Church to the king and queen of Castile, to rule and govern them, convert them to belief in Christ and the Holy Catholic Church, and give them to prosper temporally and spiritually — , this subject was not able to contain himself from supplicating with Your Majesty, most importunely, that Your Majesty not concede such license nor allow those terrible things that the tyrants did invent, pursue, and have committed against those peaceable, humble, and meek Indian peoples, who offend no person. For these are things that are iniquitous, tyrannous, and condemned, detested, and accursed by all natural, divine, and human law (though they be called "conquests"), yet which, if they be allowed, those evil men shall, most surely, commit once more. Considering, then, the perditions of infinite souls and bodies that those subjects had once perpetrated and would again, I, not being a prisoner rendered mute, deliberated to put into writing, so that Your Highness might more easily read them, some — a very few — examples that in days past I had collected from among the countless number that I could in truth declare.

And as the archbishop of Toledo, teacher of Your Highness, was bishop of Cartagena, he did ask that account of me and presented it to Your Highness, but because of the long paths of sea and land that Your Highness has traveled, and the frequent royal occupations Your Highness has had, it may be that either Your Highness did not read that account or has forgotten that Your Highness has it. And yet such is the temerity and unreasonable eagerness of those who think nothing of spilling such immense quantities of human blood and depopulating those vast lands of their natural inhabitants and possessors, killing a thousand million souls and stealing incomparable treasures, that it grows stronger every day, and so by divers paths and several feigned colors these tyrannical men importune that they be conceded or allowed said conquests (which cannot be conceded to them without violation of natural and divine law, and therefore commission of most grave mortal sins, worthy of terrible, eternal torments). Thus I thought it right to serve Your Highness with this brief and abbreviated summary of that otherwise voluminous narration of the devastations and perditions which might be, and ought to be, composed. I beg that Your Highness read it with the generosity and royal benignity that is Your Highness's wont with the works of those subjects and servants of thine who desire to serve purely and solely to further the public weal and the prosperity of the royal estate. And once Your Highness has seen the deformity of the injustice which upon those innocent people is done, destroying them and cutting them into pieces without cause or just reason for it, but rather out of mere covetousness and ambition of those who pretend to do such nefarious deeds — once this deformity has been seen, I say, and has been understood, I beg that Your Highness be kind enough to supplicate and persuade His Majesty to deny any man who might propose to undertake such noxious and detestable enterprises, and instead lay perpetual silence upon that infernal request, with such fear and terror that no man might thereafter dare even so much as name it.

This is a thing, my most high lord, which is most sorely needful and necessary so that God might make the entire estate of the royal crown of Castile prosper spiritually and temporally, and preserve it and bestow upon it blessings. Amen.

Translated by Andrew Hurley

Bernardo de Balbuena

(c. 1561 – 1627)

In Defense of Poetry

Bernardo de Balbuena was born in Valdepeñas, Spain, in 1561 or 1562 but did not arrive in Mexico until 1584, when he was in his early twenties. In Mexico he studied in the best schools and earned an advanced degree in theology; shortly thereafter he was ordained as a priest. In 1606 Balbuena made one of his many crossings between the Old and the New Worlds; he then resided in Madrid for a brief period, returning to New Spain in 1608. After spending some years in Jamaica, Balbuena was named Bishop of Puerto Rico, and it was there he died in 1627.

Balbuena lived twenty-two years in Mexico, and it is clear that he was entranced with the country and its "capital of palaces." Marcelino Menéndez y Pelayo called Balbuena the first "American" poet, and it is his heroic poem, *La Grandeza Mexicana* (1603), praising the marvels of the New World city constructed on the site of the Aztec capital, Tenochtitlán, that has kept his fame alive. The motivation for the poem was a woman Balbuena had deeply loved, who had written Balbuena asking for descriptions of the land to which her son had been summoned.

To place Balbuena in his time, it is interesting to note that he was born within two years of Shakespeare, Galileo, and Michelangelo. This was an exciting era, marked by exploration, colonization, and great literature and art. To give credence to Balbuena's claim of the "grandeur" of the colonial capital, we may remind ourselves that there was a Spanish viceroy and court in Mexico as early as 1530, along with the elegance that accompanied that milieu. The first printing press on the continent was installed in 1549, and the University of Mexico, the first university on either American continent, was founded in 1551, some seventy years before the Pilgrims arrived on the *Mayflower*. In Mexico City the Spanish had created a magnificent city of churches, palaces, government buildings, and theaters. The first plays, nearly all on religious themes, were performed in the late sixteenth century. This evidence of culture, along with the natural wonders of New Spain, greatly impressed Balbuena upon his arrival, and his awe and affection permeates *La Grandeza Mexicana*.

The first important literature of the New World came in the form of chronicles—accounts of explorations, conquests, and encounters with all the natural and human wonders that resembled nothing ever before seen—such as the accounts that begin with the letter of Christopher Columbus (Cristóbal Colón) in 1493. Many chronicles followed, among them those written by Hernán Cortés and Bernal Díaz del Castillo, along with publications by the missionaries who followed upon the explorers' heels, such as Fray Bernardino de Sahagún and Bartolomé de las Casas. Although the first modern novel, Cervantes's *Don Quijote*, was published within two years of Balbuena's master poem, the first acknowledged Mexican novel (Fernández de Lizardi's *Periquillo sarniento*) would not be written for more than two hundred years. Poetry, particularly, and plays would be the major literary genres for a large part of the colonial period.

So it is Balbuena's *Compendio apologético en alabanza de la poesía* (A Summary in Praise of Poetry), which has been favorably compared to Sir Phillip Sidney's *In Defence of Poesie*, that is pertinent here. In this treatise, the author argues that poetry has been "so maligned" that he, Balbuena, is compelled to argue its cause: "Poetry is valuable, worthy of great esteem and high praise, as in the past it has been by learned men." Echoing the tradition of his time and anticipating the intellectual formulas of Sor Juana Inés de la

Cruz, Balbuena expressed his own thoughts and opinions by quoting voluminously what great writers and men of letters had written before him. Patrick, for example, believed that "poets should be the honored of their cities, and placed in eminent positions and achieve noble rank for being the blessed and rare creatures of nature, for nothing through the centuries and ages of the world has been the equal of the perfect poet." Plato called poets "the captains and fathers of wisdom." And in *Phaedrus* he says that "noble and excellent poems are not of human but, rather, divine invention." The Alexandrian Origines "affirms that it is a certain spiritual virtue that inspires the poet and fills his thoughts with divine force and vigor." Among so many renowned figures, Balbuena, again as Sor Juana will do nearly a century later, seeks the imprimatur of saints and disciples to give weight and integrity to his own favored genre. "Not even Saint Paul was above reading the poets of his time, or including verses in his *Epistles*." "And," Balbuena writes a little later, "who among human princes has not esteemed and honored poetry? Alexander gave great praise to Cartilus—though he was a bad poet—and from among all his treasures, King Darius selected his jewel of greatest price to adorn the cover of the works of Homer. Augustus Caesar was as familiar with Virgil as if he were a companion in his empire, and Homer was of great importance to Mecenas. [. . .] And God himself, seated before a column in the tabernacle, in the midst of His people, commanded that the marvels and majesty of His hand be transformed into songs and verses, and be learned and recited by the children of Israel, so that from a tender age they be rooted in them, and conveyed from one to another, the memory of how much was owed unto Him."

Then Balbuena argues that there would be no music were it not for poetry.

Saint Isidro says that it is as ill-informed not to know music as not to know how to read. And what music is there? Without poetry, if poetry be the soul of music. [. . .] Dion says that if the gods were to speak a human language, it would be in poetry. For they spoke thusly through their oracles, giving answers in verses, and it was also in poetry that they left the ten syllables of their most supreme revelations.

And Saint Anselm, interpreting verses and confirming his opinion, says that the seven orbs of the heavens turn and revolve with the most gentle harmony and consonance, and that if here in our inferior world we are unable to hear them it is merely because of the inconvenience and nuisance, for those above us, of making them heard in the air, which is the medium through which they could reach our ears. And though the Peripatetics do not hold that this opinion is soundly based, for our purposes it is sufficient that the composition of the world be spiritual poetry and verse.

One thing cannot be denied: that music and poetry are so agreeable to God that the celestial spirits eternally and without ceasing sing to Him the hymns of glories and praise due Him. And so when, line after line, we read in the Apocalypse about songs, music, praise, and alleluias, this is not to be understood only metaphorically but as true and sonorous voice and music, as presented by Saint Augustine and Saint Thomas.

And thus, from the beginning of creation, God created his choir of celestial musicians and poets, that is, of angelic and divine spirits, and ceaselessly and never tiring of their office, they offered, and shall eternally offer, music and praise of Him.

And it is not only in this sense that we look at poetry as being very old, but even descending to more particular things, who does not know of the great antiquity and opinion that we find in divine letters, being all of them filled with hymns, canticles, and verses of gentle and lofty harmony and consonance, and being so natural to man that this poetry seems to have begun with the very beginnings.

MSP: After these arguments for divine favor, Balbuena presents less poetic arguments.

Finally, poetry is a science that from the beginnings of the world has been continuing and spreading through it, and so natural to human generality that no nation does not know it, though other sciences and policies may be lacking. And thus we see in these new Occidental worlds, where its dwellers have no branches of learning, nor know of them, that not for that do they lack poetry and songs, in which are conserved from memory to memory the ancient and famous deeds of their elders, it being impossible to conserve them entirely unless reduced to consonances and metered words. And the ancient Romans of our Spain allude to the same matter.

MSP: Having listed many famous men's praises of poetry—many more than included here—Balbuena's own appreciation follows.

And if all those from past times did not accept these tenets, it is not the fault of the art, which is capable in itself of holding a thousand secrets and divinations, but of those who with little talent and resources discredit it, throwing themselves into it with little intelligence, experience, and spirit, and without that great wealth of learning and study necessary to achieve eminence in it, maddened and led by whim and vain furor and the blind presumption that each of us has in himself regarding his talents. For nothing is more bold than ignorance, and finally it is this alone that with fire and blood wages war with a thousand strategies and boldnesses, humbling poetry with low thoughts that are unworthy of human esteem or of being heard by honest and serious ears.

But neither is it just that because of a few, others are lost, and that if the ignorant, the idiot, and the vulgar, who with mad arrogance bury their snouts in others' grain and push forward and presume to try to do what they do not understand, time, which is the assayer of all things, the touchstone of truth and the measure and weight of it, will deal out their payment and disillusion and to each the place he merits.

And so, the true appreciation is to judge each for itself, and though in man's lineage there have been many who are wicked, there is no reason that all must be reproached, nor because of many foolish verses the dignity and excellence of poetry be condemned, for in the end each will conform to its subject: divine if it be divine; honest and grave if the subject be grave and honest; or lascivious, low, and unskillful if it treats such things. [. . .]

The elegance of words; the propriety of the language; the soft and beautiful transferences; the keen, graceful, and novel modes of expression: fullness, abundance, clarity, loftiness, and delicate style; the ordinary and commonplace said in a particular and extraordinary manner; and, what is more, extraordinary, novel and difficult things in an ordinary and easy way. All this is the purview of the poet, who has the obligation to be broadly learned in all things: in prose and in verse, in one and another genre, and in all that he writes and speaks with eminence and wealth of knowledge. Nor must any think that a poem without soul, a sonnet dreamed, a *romance** without dream, will wreathe his brow with laurel and bestow upon him the immortal crown and renown of the poet. [. . .]

And finally, poetry is and has been, since the beginning of the world, the joy and solace of that world, so pleasant and sweet that its harmonic notes compose and entertain the soul, restore the spirit, mitigate anger, lighten labors, are company in loneliness, and, as Macrobius says, awaken virtue and entertain: birds warble it; swans sing it; turtle doves coo it; larks, nightingales, linnets, canaries, and sparrows all trill it in counterpoint. To all it is delight and pleasure: dolphins in the sea, horses in war, travelers in the desert, the shepherd with his flock, the sailor at the helm, the fisherman with his nets, the official in his tasks, the honored at the feast, the nun in her cloister, the maiden at her handwork, the suitor in his courting, the religious in his choir. To all it is companionship, to all it is gift and consolation, to all it pleases and lifts the spirit. [. . .]

Finally, poetry is a delicious wine of the imagination, which in moderation gives joy to the spirit, a gift to comprehension, delight to fantasy, surcease to sadness, and perpetual and marvelous pleasure to its practitioners, for, as the refrain says, *He who sings to his ills, frightens them away*. [. . .]

Poetry is relief and entertainment to other more serious cares. Because, what taste is there so sour and melancholic, what blood so cold and thinned that a marvelous epic or heroic poem will not uplift by reading in it the lofty and sublime deeds of ancient heroes and famous captains, of the kings and princes of the world? And if he be truthful, what man does the lyric or melic not delight?

And so Fray Luis de León says very well [. . .] that poetry is nothing other than a painting that speaks, and all its study and perfection consists in, and

*A Spanish verse form.

is an imitation of, nature: a caution and warning that few of our Castillian poets have heeded; instead, rashly writing on matters of love, they followed the same steps by which they believed they would reach the heights of refined expression; but in following those steps, some wander very far from the office of good poets. For excellence is achieved not in writing love couplets but in serious, uncorrupted, sententious works permeated with morality and philosophy.

And thus, those who in this livery emerge honest, grave, and moderate, and are born not of rash spirit but of thought leavened with art, why should they be denied the good they brought with them? For in the end they are the happy and blessed creations of human reason. And as Hieronymus Román [Saint Jerome] says, such poets were praised in ancient times and forever have deserved to be, and are compared in hieroglyphic figures to the bee: for in the same way that she puts care and solicitude in making her honeycombs, so do poets give of the sweetness of their expression with great invention and artifice.

They were crowned with laurel, a tree that never loses its freshness, and neither does the fame of those men ever wither or grow old. They were also crowned with ivy, a vine that with uncommon artifice wraps and curls itself around trees and houses, so tightly clinging and bound to them that once they are entwined the tree and house will collapse and crumble within the vine before the vine releases its hold. In which one notes the artful way that poets devise and organize their books, and how their memory is perpetuated, enduring longer than the empires and kingdoms of the world. As we see in Homer and Virgil, who wrote of the Greeks and Romans, both of whose kingdoms ended but the poets live and will live on as long as the world is peopled with wise men and not beasts. And these have been Román's words.

And so by this account, poetry is in itself most capable of all the *grandezas* that we have assigned to it; the fault, therefore, lies not in the character or science of poetry but in the choices of its practitioners, who select baser occasions and subjects in which to employ themselves and make their names.

And though I know and recognize this, and also that what I write here [*La Grandeza*] is not completely divine, it is at least honest and serious and on a heroic theme, and not base in its design or outside the laws and conditions of art. [. . .] But for now it is sufficient recommendation for these brief discourses, and for any misgiving that may have arisen regarding them, that they lie not in the subject, for that treats an illustrious city, head and crown of these Occidental worlds, famous for its name, renowned for its situation and location and for its ancient and present power, known and respected in the world and for its many qualities worthy of being celebrated as unique and singular. And for a heroic and pious Prelate who, setting aside for now virtues of valor, saintliness, and nobility more properly his than of the Sun the light radiating from it, is most worthy Archbishop and spiritual head of it.

So my poetry in grave and heroic style treats the most noble, the richest, and most populous city in this new America, and of which it is the spiritual supreme pastor and governor. For if this subject is worthy of noble comprehension, and if with the little or much knowledge at my command I allocate to it and endow and treat it with nothing that will detract or offend — either its majesty, or my faculty, or grave and serious ears — it does not seem to me that it will be against my profession and habit to demonstrate on an occasion such as this that also when young I passed through the principles of rhetoric and emerged upon the threshold of poetry, nor is it just that in any time one person disdain what in others may be a virtue.

"And thus, not to carry these thoughts further, I conclude, with a desire to give balm to mine, with the distich of Ovid in the tenth elegy of his first book:

> *Scindentur vestes, gemmai frangetur, et aurum,*
> *Carmina quam tribuent fama peremnis erit.*

> All things, over the course of time, will come to an end, diverse Treasures, gold, raiment, jewels, but not the name immortalized in verse."

Translated by Margaret Sayers Peden

Sor Juana Inés de la Cruz

(c. 1651 – 1695)

[FROM]

Response to Sor Filotea

In 1691 Sor Juana, besieged by a church hierarchy demanding that she renounce her worldly writing, composed the "Respuesta a Sor Filotea," the first document in our hemisphere to defend a woman's right to teach, to study, and to write. As an intellectual woman in a world in which male dominance and, especially ecclesiastical male dominance, was the rule, Sor Juana's art, her beauty, and her spirit led her inexorably toward the confrontation that produced the "Respuesta." That passionate yet icily rational outburst was followed by four years of nearly total silence. She acceded to the insistent demands of the Church hierarchy; she surrendered her books and her collections of musical and mathematical instruments; she ended her communication with the world of the viceregal court; she reaffirmed her vows to the Church, signed at least two documents in her own blood; and in 1695, during a devastating plague, in which all evidence confirms her heroic devotion to her stricken sisters, she died. [. . .]

Even three centuries after Sor Juana's birth, two almost contemporaneous documents remain as the principal sources for biographical information: the "Respuesta" itself and the imprimatur—more a biographical eulogy than a *nihil obstat*—issued by the Spanish priest Diego Calleja on the occasion of the publication of Sor Juana's *Fama y Obras Póstumas* (Madrid, 1700). [. . .]

Briefly, the facts about Sor Juana's life are the following, although we begin with some uncertainty. [. . .] Sor Juana lived in Nepantla, the tiny village of her birth, either five or eight years, depending which birth date one accepts. While she probably did not know her father, the influence of her grandfather, a man with a considerable library and three remarkably independent daughters, is widely acknowledged. It is known that in the year of his death, 1656, Sor Juana was sent to Mexico City to live with her well-to-do aunt and uncle. [. . .] We know virtually nothing about the years that Juana Inés lived with those relatives, the Matas, in Mexico City. We do know that the word of Sor Juana's unusual intelligence spread rapidly. Calleja records how Don Antonio Sebastián de Toledo, Marqués de Mancera and viceroy of New Spain, called together the most learned men in the land—forty theologians, philosophers, mathematicians, historians, poets, and humanists—to examine the young woman of whom everyone was talking. The viceroy reported to Calleja "that in the manner that a royal galleon might fend off the attacks of small canoes, so did Juana extricate herself from the questions, arguments, and objections these many men, each in his specialty, directed to her." In addition, Sor Juana quickly won the affection of the vicereine, and spent two years in the viceregal palace as her protégée. Those vitally important years probably constitute the most serious lacuna in reconstructing the poet's life, and must be derived from her writing.

In 1667, for reasons that have not been ascertained, Sor Juana entered the convent of the Carmelitas Descalzas. Whether for reasons of health—as Méndez Plancarte, the editor of her *Obras completas* believes—or because the rules of the order were too strict for her tastes—as others have argued—she remained only three months with the Carmelites. In 1669, however, Sor Juana made her definite decision and entered the convent of San Jerónimo, where she studied and wrote until the crisis of the "Respuesta" in 1691, and where she lived until her death in 1695. [. . .]

Of one thing we can be sure. Sor Juana was the target of envy and jealousy throughout her adult life. Those themes occur again and again in her poems, and are a major concern in the "Repuesta." The injunctions of the obey your pastoral suggestions, as your direction, which may be inferred from the premise and arguments of my Letter. For I know well that your most sensible warning is not directed against it, but rather against those worldly matters of which I have written. And thus I had hoped with the Letter to make amends for any lack of application you may (with great reason) have inferred from others of my writings; and, speaking more particularly, I confess to you with all the candor of which you are deserving, and with the truth and clarity which are the natural custom in me, that my not having written often of sacred matters was not caused by disaffection or by want of application, but by the abundant fear and reverence due those Sacred Letters, knowing myself incapable of their comprehension and unworthy of their employment. [. . .] For how then would I have dared take in my unworthy hands these verses, defying gender, age, and above all, custom? And thus I confess that many times this fear has plucked my pen from my hand and has turned my thoughts back toward the very same reason from which they had wished to be born: which obstacle did not impinge upon profane matters, for a heresy against art is not punished by the Holy Office but by the judicious with derision, and by critics with censure, and censure, *just or unjust, is not to be feared,* as it does not forbid the taking of communion or hearing of mass, and offers me little or no cause for anxiety, because in the opinion of those who defame my art, I have neither the obligation to know nor the aptitude to triumph. If, then, I err, I suffer neither blame nor discredit: I suffer no blame, as I have no obligation; no discredit, as I have no possibility of triumphing — *and no one is obliged to do the impossible.* And, in truth, I have written nothing except when compelled and constrained, and then only to give pleasure to others; not alone without pleasure of my own, but with absolute repugnance, for I have never deemed myself one who has any worth in letters or the wit necessity demands of one who would write; and thus my customary response to those who press me, above all in sacred matters, is, what capacity of reason have I? what application? what resources? what rudimentary knowledge of such matters beyond that of the most superficial scholarly degrees? Leave these matters to those who understand them; I wish no quarrel with the Holy Office, for I am ignorant, and I tremble that I may express some proposition that will cause offense or twist the true meaning of some scripture. I do not study to write, even less to teach — which in one like myself were unseemly pride — but only to the end that if I study, I will be ignorant of less. This is my response, and these are my feelings.

I have never written of my own choice, but at the urging of others, to whom with reason I might say, *You have compelled me*.[11] But one truth I shall not deny (first, because it is well known to all, and second, because although it has not worked in my favor, God has granted me the mercy of loving truth above all else), which is that from the moment I was first illuminated by the light of reason, my inclination toward letters has been so vehement, so over-powering, that not even the admonitions of others — and I have suffered many — nor my own meditations — and they have not been few — have been sufficient to cause me to forswear this natural impulse that God placed in me: the Lord God knows why, and for what purpose. And He knows that I have prayed that He dim the light of my reason, leaving only that which is needed to keep His Law, for there are those who would say that all else is unwanted in a woman, and there are even those who would hold that such knowledge does injury. And my Holy Father knows too that as I have been unable to achieve this (my prayer has not been answered), I have sought to veil the light of my reason — along with my name — and to offer it up only to Him who bestowed it upon me, and He knows that none other was the cause for my entering into Religion, notwithstanding that the spiritual exercises and company of a community were repugnant to the freedom and quiet I desired for my studious endeavors. And later, in that community, the Lord God knows — and, in the world, only the one who must know — how dili-gently I sought to obscure my name, and how this was not permitted, saying it was temptation: and so it would have been. If it were in my power, lady, to repay you in some part what I owe you, it might be done by telling you this thing which had never before passed my lips, except to be spoken to the one who should hear it. It is my hope that by having opened wide to you the doors of my heart, by having made patent to you its most deeply hidden secrets, you will deem my confidence not unworthy of the debt I owe to your most august person and to your most uncommon favors.

[. . .]

---

11. II Corinthians 12:4.

Oh, that each of us — I, being ignorant, the first — should take the measure of our talents before we study or, more important, write with the covetous ambition to equal and even surpass others, how little spirit we should have for it, and how may errors we should avoid, and how many tortured intellects of which we have experience, we should have had no experience! And I place my own ignorance in the forefront of all these, for if I knew all I should, I would not write. And I protest that I do so only to obey you; and with such apprehension that you owe me more that I have taken up my pen in fear than you would have owed had I presented you more perfect works. But it is well that they go to your correction. Cross them out, tear them up, reprove me, and I shall appreciate that more than all the vain applause others may offer. *That just men shall correct me in mercy, and shall reprove me; but let not the oil of the sinner fatten my head.*[12]

[. . .]

If the offense is to be found in the *Atenagórica* letter, was that letter anything other than the simple expression of my feeling, written with the implicit permission of our Holy Mother Church? For if the Church, in her most sacred authority, does not forbid it, why must others do so? That I proffered an opinion contrary to that of de Vieyra was audacious, but, as a Father, was it not audacious that he speak against the three Holy Fathers of the Church? My reason, such as it is, is it not as unfettered as his, as both issue from the same source? Is his opinion to be considered as a revelation, as a principle of Holy Faith, that we must accept blindly? Furthermore, I maintained at all times the respect due such a virtuous man, a respect in which his defender was sadly wanting, ignoring the phrase of Titus Lucius: *Respect is companion to the arts.* I did not touch a thread of the robes of the Society of Jesus; nor did I write for other than the consideration of the person who suggested that I write. And, according to Pliny, *how different the condition of one who writes from that of one who merely speaks.* Had I believed the letter was to be published I would not have been so inattentive. If, as the censor says, the letter is heretical, why does he not denounce it? And with that he would be avenged, and I content, for, which is only seemly, I esteem more highly my reputation as a Catholic and obedient daughter of the Holy Mother Church than all the

12. Psalm 140:5.

approbation due a learned woman. If the letter is rash, and he does well to criticize it, then laugh, even if with the laugh of the rabbit, for I have not asked that he approve; as I was free to dissent from de Vieyra, so will anyone be free to oppose my opinion.

[. . .]

Then if I turn my eyes to the oft-chastised faculty of making verses — which is in me so natural that I must discipline myself that even this letter not be written in that form — I might cite those lines, *All I wished to express took the form of verse.* And seeing that so many condemn and criticize this ability, I have conscientiously sought to find what harm may be in it, and I have not found it, but, rather, I see verse acclaimed in the mouths of the Sibyls, sanctified in the pens of the Prophets, especially King David, of whom the exalted Expositer my beloved Father says (explicating the measure of his meters): *in the manner of Horace and Pindar, now it hurries along in iambs, now it rings in alcaic, now swells in sapphic, then arrives in broken feet.* The greater part of the Holy Books are in meter, as is the Book of Moses; and those of Job (as Saint Isidore states in his *Etymologiae*) are in heroic verse. Solomon wrote the Canticle of Canticles in verse; and Jeremiah, his Lamentations. And so, says Cassiodorus: *All poetic expression had as its source the Holy Scriptures.* For not only does our Catholic Church not disdain verse, it employs verse in its hymns, and recites the lines of Saint Ambrose, Saint Thomas, Saint Isidore, and others. Saint Bonaventure was so taken with verse that he writes scarcely a page where it does not appear. It is readily apparent that Saint Paul had studied verse, for he quotes and translates verses of Aratus: *For in him we live, and move, and are.*[13] And he quotes also that verse of Parmenides: *The Cretans are always liars, evil beasts, slothful bellies.*[14] Saint Gregory Nazianzen argues in elegant verses the questions of matrimony and virginity. And, how should I tire? The Queen of Wisdom, Our Lady, with Her sacred lips, intoned the Canticle of the Magnificat; and having brought forth this example, it would be offensive to add others that were profane, even those of the most serious and learned men, for this alone is more than sufficient confirmation; and even though Hebrew elegance could not be compressed into

13. Acts 17:28.
14. Titus 1:12.

Latin measure, for which reason, although the sacred translator, more atten-
tive to the importance of the meaning, omitted the verse, the Psalms retain
the number and divisions of verses, and what harm is to be found in them?
For misuse is not the blame of art, but rather of the evil teacher who perverts
the arts, making of them the snare of the devil; and this occurs in all the arts
and sciences.

And if the evil is attributed to the fact that a women employs them, we
have seen how many have done so in praiseworthy fashion; what then is the
evil in my being a woman? I confess openly my own baseness and meanness,
but I judge that no couplet of mine has been deemed indecent. Furthermore, I have never written of my own will, but under the pleas and injunctions of others; to such a degree that the only piece I remember having written for my own pleasure was a little trifle they called *El sueño.* That letter,
lady, which you so greatly honored, I wrote more with repugnance than any
other emotion; both by reason of the fact that it treated sacred matters, for
which (as I have stated) I hold such reverent awe, and because it seems to
wish to impugn, a practice for which I have natural aversion; and I believe
that had I foreseen the blessed destiny to which it was fated — for like a second Moses I had set it adrift, naked, on the waters of the Nile of silence,
where you, a princess, found and cherished it — I believe, I reiterate, that
had I known, the very hands of which it was born would have drowned it,
out of the fear that these clumsy scribblings from my ignorance appear
before the light of your great wisdom; by which one knows the munificence
of your kindness, for your goodwill applauds precisely what your reason
must wish to reject. For as fate cast it before your doors, so exposed, so
orphaned, that it fell to you even to give it a name, I must lament that among
other deformities it also bears the blemish of haste, both because of the
unrelenting ill-heath I suffer, and for the profusion of duties imposed on me
by obedience, as well as the want of anyone to guide me in my writing and
the need that it all come from my hand, and, finally, because the writing went
against my nature and I wished only to keep my promise to one whom I
could not disobey, I could not find the time to finish properly, and thus I
failed to include whole treatises and many arguments that presented themselves to me, but which I omitted in order to put an end to the writing —
many, that had I known the letter was to be printed, I would not have

excluded, even if merely to satisfy some objections that have since arisen and which could have been refuted. But I shall not be so ill-mannered as to place such indecent objects before the purity of your eyes, for it is enough that my ignorance be an offense in your sight, without the need of entrusting to it the effronteries of others. But if in their audacity these latter should wing their way to you (and they are of such little weight that this will happen) then you will command what I am to do; for, if it does not run contrary to your will, my defense shall be not to take up my pen, for I deem that one affront need not occasion another, if one recognizes the error in the very place it lies concealed. [. . .] And thus in what little of mine that has been printed, neither the use of my name, nor even consent for the printing, was given by my own counsel, but by the license of another who lies outside my domain, as was also true with the printing of the *Antenagórica* letter, and only a few *Exercises of the Incarnation* and *Offerings of the Sorrows* were printed for the public devotions with my pleasure but without my name; of which I am sending some few copies that (if you so desire) you may distribute them among your sisters, the nuns of the holy community, as well as in that city. I send but one copy of the *Sorrows* because the others have been exhausted and I could find no other copy. I wrote them long ago, solely for the devotions of my sisters, and later they were spread abroad; and their contents are disproportionate as regards my unworthiness and my ignorance, and they profited that they touched on matters of our exalted Queen; for I cannot explain what it is that inflames the coldest heart when one refers to the Most Holy Mary. It is my only desire, esteemed lady, to remit to you works worthy of your virtue and wisdom; as the poet said:

> Though strength may falter, good will must be praised.
> In this, I believe, that gods will be content.

If I ever write again, my scribbling will always find its way to the haven of your holy feet and the certainty of your correction, for I have no other jewel with which to pay you, and, in the lament of Seneca, he who had once bestowed benefices has committed himself to continue; and so you must be repaid out of your own munificence, for only in this way shall I with dignity be freed from debt and avoid that the words of that same Seneca come to pass: *It is contemptible to be surpassed in benefices.* For in his gallantry the gener-

José Joaquín Fernández de Lizardi

(1776 – 1827)

The Itching Parrot

José Joaquín Fernández de Lizardi was born in Mexico City in 1771. There he attended the University of Mexico, then worked in government service in Taxco, where in 1812 he surrendered that city's defenses to the revolutionary forces of José María Morelos. As a result he was captured by the royalists and returned to Mexico City as a rebel sympathizer, though he was freed when he convinced the magistrate that he surrendered the arms only to avoid bloodshed. In Mexico City he established the newspaper that was to give him the pseudonym by which he became known: *El Pensador Mexicano*, the Mexican Thinker; a second paper, *El Conductor Eléctrico* (the Electric Conductor) is also an apt sobriquet for this free thinker.

Fernández de Lizardi was a journalist, essayist, novelist, political pamphleteer, fabulist, dramatist, and general gadfly. He was twice imprisoned and once excommunicated for his writing but continued to produce controversial articles until the time of his death by tuberculosis in 1827. A number of his works were published following his death, including two novels and a series of moralistic essays, but his fame today rests, unequivocally, on the novel *El periquillo sarniento*, published serially in 1816 and posthumously, in its entirety, in 1836. This picaresque tale is the first novel published in Latin America and as such continues to be of interest to readers and scholars alike as a prominent milestone in the history of the Spanish-language novel. The

Periquillo contains very little commentary on the craft of writing—Fernández was far too active a social critic to meditate on literary style—though he does make the case, of all things, for good penmanship as a requisite of writing, a strange premise that looks back to the work of Sor Juana Inés de la Cruz and forward to the musings of the contemporary Margo Glantz.

There is a strange side note to this first Mexican novel: its first translation into English. That appeared in 1942 under the title *The Itching Parrot*; the translator—here a little-known literary curiosity—was Katherine Anne Porter. In her thirty-two-page introduction to the translation, this is how Porter refers to Fernández de Lizardi.

> The outlook was pretty thin for such as our hero. But he was to prove extra-ordinarily a child of his time, and his subsequent career was not the result of any personal or family plan, but was quite literally created by a movement of history, a true world movement, in which he was caught up and spun about and flung down again. His life story cannot be separated in any particular from the history of the Mexican Revolutionary period. He was born at the peak of the Age of Reason, in the year that the thirteen states of North America declared themselves independent of England. When he was a year old, the United States government decreed religious freedom. In Mexico the Inquisition was still in power, and the Spanish clergy in that country had fallen into a state of corruption perhaps beyond anything known before or since. The viceregal court was composed entirely of Spanish nobles who lived in perpetual luxurious exile; the Indian people were their natural serfs, the mixed Indian and Spanish were slowly forming a new intractable, unpredictable race, and all were ruled extravagantly and unscrupulously by a long succession of viceroys so similar and so unremarkable it is not worth while to recall their names.

This paragraph is a good summary of the Mexican condition, and her introductory essay reveals her exploration of the period and specifically of the life of de Lizardi. What is not revealed is that from the title page on ("Translated from the Spanish, and with an Introduction by Katherine Anne Porter") there is no mention of Eugene Pressly, almost certainly the author of the translation that Porter edited, and her husband for five years.

One further bibliographical note: *The Itching Parrot* omitted de Lizardi's slow and didactic moralizing chapters, arguably improving the book for modern expectations. The discriminating reader, however, may make that judgment for himself since a new and complete translation by David Frye and Nancy Vogeley has recently been published under the title *The Mangy Parrot: The Life and Times of Periquillo Sarniento, Written by Himself for His Children.*

That title segues to the stated *cause d'etre* of de Lizardi's novel: an apology for and exculpation of a life of roguery, trickery, and deception. The unstated—at least within the novel—purpose was, of course, didactic and moralizing, a scathing protest against the terrible conditions of the poor, the hypocrisy of the wealthy, and the vices of the clergy.

The first excerpt from the Porter-Pressly translation is Pedro Sarmiento's plea to his children, written so that being "warned by my example," they will fare better in their lives than he in his. He does address the style of his pages, the matter of who shall be qualified to read them, and the benefits of his maxims: a rather broad outline for social and political treatises throughout the centuries.

The pages included from chapter two describe the way his "good master" expressed himself and how he wrote. It is here that de Lizardi, through Pedro Sarmiento, discusses the virtues of the basics of writing. The master's accidents of punctuation lead to his dismissal. The priest's decision is based on "your bad writing," a strong lesson to Periquillo. (It is in school that Pedro Sarmiento becomes Periquillo Sarniento, his not uncommon last name changed by the shift of one letter to "mangy, or itchy," and the diminutive of Pedro—Pedrito or Pedrillo—easily morphed into "little parrot," Periquillo, because of the bright yellow and green he often wears to class.)

Chapter five is devoted to the matter of Periquillo's choice of careers—his father urging him not to become trapped in the unproductive careers of *belles lettres* or poet. He did, however, make a new friend, "one Lizardi, a sorry writer . . . known to the public as 'the Mexican Thinker,' who discusses his own flaws as a writer." It is to this de Lizardi that Pedro Sarmiento gives the notebooks that compose the pages of *The Itching Parrot*, and who will do Sarmiento the favor of seeing them published. It is he who composes the

Epilogue, bringing this picaresque tale to its end. "The Thinker Relates the Rest, Up to the Death of Our Hero, His Burial, and Other Things That Lead the Reader by the Hand Up to the End of This True History."

PROLOGUE

Being prostrate in my bed these many months, battling with doctors and mortal decay, awaiting with resignation the day on which, obedient to the mandate of Divine Providence, you, my dear children, must close my eyes, it has occurred to me to leave you a written account of the not unusual events of my life, in order that you may know how to guard against and save yourselves from the many dangers that threaten and sometimes overtake man in the course of his days.

I desire that by reading this you learn to avoid many errors here confessed, by me and by others, and that, warned by my example, you may not expose yourselves to such ill-treatment as I have suffered through my own fault. Be assured it is better to profit by other men's disillusions than by your own. Especially I beg you be not scandalized at the disorders of my youth, which I shall recount without hiding anything and with shame enough; for, since you are exposed to the same dangers, my desire is to instruct you and save you from the reefs whereon my youth was shattered so many times.

Do not think that the reading of my history will be too tedious for you, for I well know that variety delights the understanding and I shall manage to avoid the monotony and dullness of style that usually vexes readers. Thus sometimes you will mark me serious and sententious as a Cato, at others as trivial and buffoonish as a Bertoldo. At times you will discover fragments of erudition and bits of eloquence in my discourse; and, again, a popular style mixed with the proverbs and mannerisms of the common people. Also, I promise you this shall be done without affectation or pedantry; accordingly as a thing may recur in my memory it shall be put immediately upon paper, this method seeming to me the most suited to our natural levity.

Lastly, I command and charge you that these notebooks leave not your hands, in order that they may not be subjected to the calumny of fools or dishonest men; but, if you should weaken and lend them sometime, I beg you not to lend them to that kind of men; nor to hypocritical old females; nor to avaricious priests, who make profit of living and dead parishioners alike; nor to bungling doctors and lawyers; not to thievish scriveners; solicitors, counsellors, or attorneys; nor to merchants, usurers; nor to first born heirs; nor to fathers and mothers who are lax in the training of their families; nor to stupid, superstitious, pious women; nor to mercenary judges; nor to knavish constables; nor to tyrannous jailers; nor to patchwork poets and writers like me; nor to boastful, affected officers and soldiers; nor to the greedy, stupid, proud, rich, oppressors of men; nor to the poor who are so because of their laziness or bad conduct; nor to feigning beggars; nor lend them either to the girls who rent themselves, nor to the young women who gad about, nor to the old women who paint their faces, nor —. But this list grows long: it is enough to say you should not lend them even for a minute to any one of those people whom you foresee proscribed by what they would read; for, in spite of what I say in my prologue, the moment they see their secret selves portrayed by my pen, the moment they read some opinion new to them or not comfortable with their abandoned, depraved ideas, that same instant they will tag me a fool, pretend to be shocked by my discourses, and there may even be those who will pretend I am a heretic and denounce me for such, even though I may be long since gone to dust. So great is the power of malice, of prejudice, of ignorance!

Now then, either read my notebooks yourselves only, or in case you lend them let it be only to truly honest men, for although as weak mortals they have erred and still may err, they will accept the burden of truth without feeling themselves offended, knowing that I speak of no one in particular, but of all those who trespass the limits of justice. The former, if in the end they read my work, you may be sure of putting to flight when they take offense or laugh at it by saying, "Why are you disturbed? Why do you scoff? This man tells of an intemperate life under another name than yours."

My children, after my death you will read this story for the first time. Direct your prayers for me then to the Throne of Mercy. Take warning from my mad errors; do not let yourselves be deceived by the falseness of men; observe the maxims I teach, remembering I learned them at cost of very painful experiences; never praise my work, for my desire to benefit you had been the chief motive for it; and, keeping these considerations in mind, begin to read —

CHAPTER 2

Poll Tells about His Entering School, the Progress He Made, and Other Matters Which He Who Reads, Hears Read, or Asks about Shall Know.

My father grew angry, my mother wept, and I did a pile of complaining and sulking, sobbed, and shed a thousand tears; but nothing availed to make my father revoke his decision. I was shut up in school whether I would or no.

The master was a very honorable man, but he lacked the qualities necessary for his profession. In the first place, he was a poor man and had taken up this work out of pure necessity, without consulting his inclination or ability. It was to be expected he would be as he was, displeased with and even ashamed of his occupation.

Men believe — I don't know why — that boys, because they are boys, neither understand nor enjoy listening to men's conversation; and, confident in this error, they are careless in talking about things that sometime or other the children throw back in their very faces. Then they learn that the young are both curious and observant. I was this kind of child, and I did exactly what might be expected. My master seated me next to him, perhaps because of my father's special recommendation or because I was the best off for clothing among his pupils: I do not know what there is about a good appearance that is respected even among boys. Taking advantage of my nearness to him, I lost not a word of his talk with his friends. Once I heard him say to one of them, "Only hellish poverty could have driven me into schoolkeeping. So much damned boy is no life for me. How wild they are, and what fools! No matter what I do, I cannot see one progressing. Ah, damn such an evil occupation! To be a schoolmaster is the worst trick the devil can play on us!"

Thus my good master expressed himself, and by his words you may judge the simplicity of his heart, the little talent he had for and the low concept he had formed of a profession so noble and commendable in itself. For to teach and direct youth is a charge of high dignity; kings and governments have heaped learned professors with honors and privileges. But my poor master knew nothing of all this, and so it was to be expected he would form a bad opinion of such an honorable profession.

In the second place, he lacked, as I have said, a turn for it, or what is called talent. He had a kind heart; it was distasteful to him to punish anyone: and this soft character made him overindulgent with his pupils. He rarely scolded them harshly and more rarely chastised them. In his judgment, the ruler and discipline were of little use. The boys were in their glory, I among them; for we did what we pleased with impunity.

On the other hand, my master lacked entirely the ability to fulfill his title. He knew how to read enough to understand and make himself understood at most; but not enough to teach. And if he read so badly, how did he write? A bit worse; and it could not have been otherwise, for you cannot build a firm structure upon a weak foundation. It is true he had his points in what is called penmanship: he wrote a pretty hand; but of punctuation he knew nothing. He adorned his writings with periods, commas, interrogation marks, and other things of the sort; but without order, method, or understanding, so that things turned out so ridiculously that it had been better for him not to have put in even a single comma. Like the donkey that played the flute by accident, he who tries to do something he does not always understand how to do will hit the mark sometimes, but almost always he will spoil all he attempts, as did my master in this particular. Of course, he made mistakes whenever he wrote anything; and it would have been none the worse if only ridiculous mistakes had resulted from his unfortunate punctuation, but sometimes scandalous blasphemies came out.

He had a beautiful image of the Virgin of the Immaculate Conception and he wrote underneath it a motto which, of course, should read:

Mary conceived without stain of original sin! No one can deny it.

But the unhappy man erred as was his habit in writing the punctuation marks, and wrote a devilish extravagance worthy of his being hanged had he done it with the slightest intention, for he wrote:

Mary conceived without stain of original sin? No; one can deny it.

You see now how a person who has never learned to punctuate is apt to make thousands of mistakes, and how necessary it is for you to be careful of your children regarding this.

Surely you already know what I learned from such a skillful teacher. Nothing, of course. I was a year under his care, and in that time I learned to read running, as my candid preceptor called it, although I read even at a gallop; for, as he paid no attention to such puerilities as teaching us to read according to punctuation, we jumped the periods, parentheses, exclamation points, and other little obstacles of this sort more lightly than cats; and this my master, and others like him, extolled.

[. . .]

As to my progress in school, I say there was none, and so it would have been always if a mere accident had not freed me from this master. It happened one day a priest came in with a child to leave in the master's care. He talked with the master a while, and as he was taking leave he observed the little motto I have mentioned, looked at it attentively, took out an eyeglass, read it again, tried to rub away the marks, particularly after the "No," believing they might be flyspecks, and when he satisfied himself they were indeed written, he asked, "Who wrote this?"

My good master answered that he himself had written it. The priest grew indignant and said, "And you, what do you mean by writing such a thing?"

"Father," my master answered, stuttering, "I-I meant to say that Our Blessed Lady was conceived without stain of original sin and no one can deny it."

"Then, my friend," the priest replied, "you meant to say so; for what one reads here is a scandalous error. But, since it is only the result of your bad writing, take the penholder and all the cotton from the inkstand and erase, this moment, before I go, this wicked motto; and if you do not know how to use punctuation, leave it out, for it will do less harm if you trust your letters and all you write to the discretion of your readers, without a drop of punctuation, rather than write insults and blasphemies like this one by doing what you do not know how to do."

My master, poor man, hurriedly and shamefacedly erased the fatal verse in front of the priest and us. As soon as he concluded his tacit retraction, the priest proceeded, "I am going to take my nephew away, for he is blind because of his youth and you because of your ignorance; and if the blind lead the blind, as you must have heard, the two are bound to fall over a precipice. You have a good heart and good deportment, but these qualities in themselves are not enough to make good fathers, good tutors, good masters for youth. Therefore, find another occupation, for if I see this school open again I shall advise the Head Master and have him revoke your license, if you have any. Goodbye." [. . .]

CHAPTER 5

[. . .]

About this time, my friends visited me and by chance I made a new friend, one de Lizardi, Carlos's godfather at his confirmation, a sorry writer in your motherland, known to the public as "the Mexican Thinker," under which pen name he distinguished himself in these bitter times. During the time I have known and treated with him, I have noted in him little learning, less talent, and, lastly, no merit — I speak with my accustomed frankness; but, in exchange for these faults, I know he is not deceitful nor false, not a flatterer nor a hypocrite. To me it is evident he does not hold himself learned or virtuous; he knows his own faults, realizes, confesses, and detests them. He knows what he really is; full of ignorance and pride, blinded by these defects and not always realizing it. Once when some learned men praised his work in his presence, I heard him say, "Gentlemen, do not be deceived. I am neither wise nor erudite. I know well what is needed to fulfill those titles, but my works deceive you when you read them for the first time. All of them are but tinsel. I am ashamed to see in print errors I did not notice at the time I wrote. My easy way of writing does not prove authority. Often I write in the midst of the distraction of my family and friends. This does not justify my errors, for I should correct my writing carefully, or else write not at all, following Virgil's and Horace's examples. But once I have written, I realize that by natural inclination I have no patience to read over, to rewrite, erase, amend, or consider my work carefully; I confess I do nothing as it should be done, but I firmly believe learned men will excuse me, attributing to the heat of my imagination the culpable haste of my pen. I speak only of the judgment of the wise, for that of fools does not matter to me." On hearing these words from the Thinker, I marked him for my friend, certain that he was an honest man and, if he erred sometimes, it was more because of his disturbed mind than depraved will; I numbered him among my true friends, and he won my affection in such manner that I made him master of my most secret confidences; we have loved each other so constantly that I can truly say I am one and the same with the Thinker and he with me.

One day when I was very sick, when I was scarcely able to write in this my little history, he came to visit me, and with my wife sitting on the edge of my bed, you children gathered around her, realizing myself so exhausted by my sufferings that I could write no more, I said to him, "Take these notebooks, so that my children may benefit by them when my days are ended." I left my friend the Thinker my last messages and these notebooks, so that he might correct them and annotate them, for I find myself very ill.

Epilogue

[. . .]

According to the special charge he had made, after waiting two days, we went on with the funeral, doing him honor in all solemnity; and when this was done the corpse was taken to the Campo Santo and given burial. The tomb was sealed with a white marble slab, on which was carved the epitaph the deceased himself had composed before his death.

HIC IACET
PETRVS SARMIENTO
(VVLGO)
PERIQVILLO SARNIENTO
PECCATOR VITA
NIHIL MORTA
OVISQVIS ADES
DEVM ORA
VT
IN AETERNVM VALEAT

HERE LIES

PEDRO SARMIENTO

COMMONLY KNOWN AS

THE ITCHING PARROT,

IN LIFE

A SINNER:

IN DEATH, NOTHING.

PASSER-BY, WHOEVER YOU MAY BE,

PRAY GOD GRANT HIM

ETERNAL REST.

Translated by Katherine Anne Porter

Enrique González Martínez

(1871 – 1952)

The Death of the Swan?

Modernismo. Not to be confused with English-language Modernism. As Mexican writing—and Latin American writing in general—developed during the nineteenth century, it had, with some predictable time delays, followed European models. The impact of *modernismo*, therefore, cannot be over-emphasized, as it is considered the first "original" literary movement of Latin America, though it, too—since there is so little new under the sun—developed from the French schools of Parnassianism and Symbolism.

The period of *modernismo* has been dated rather specifically, from approximately 1888 to around 1910, though signs of the movement can be perceived in the early 1880s and easily found long after 1910. Those boundaries arise from the dates of two publications. The first was *Azul* (Blue), a highly influential collection of poems by the primary figure of *modernismo*, the Nicaraguan poet Rubén Darío. Hence the rather too neat "beginning" of the movement. Similarly, its equally too-neat demise dates from the publication of a poem entitled "Tuércele el cuello del cisne," written by one of *modernismo*'s early practitioners, the Mexican Enrique González Martínez, in which, after some reconsiderations, he argues the case for "wringing the neck of the swan."

Although González Martínez is guilty of some of the excesses he berates in his poem, and though it has been argued that the poem was not intended

to sound the death knell of such an important, American-born, literary movement, it is difficult *not* to read in its lines González Martínez's rejection of its
less attractive characteristics.

Primarily a poetic movement—the novel of the turn of the century was
under the influence of realism and naturalism—*modernismo* produced some
great poets across Latin America, among them the Cuban José Martí, Darío
himself, and the Argentine Leopoldo Lugones. The positive effects of Darío's
innovations were a revitalizing experimentation with form, meter, and versi-
fication, all of which he effected with great élan. At the same time, much of
the work of the poets of this era was characterized by an immoderate fondness
for the exquisite—and subsequent rejection of "the vulgar"—for synesthesia
(see Darío's own "Sinfonía en gris mayor," or "Symphony in Gray Major"), for
idolization of a porcelain-figurine female, and for an escapism that glorified
oriental and medieval themes and décor. Lesser poets carried the superficial
qualities of *modernismo* into excesses of *preciosité*, and the writing of the
period became filled with princesses and blue lakes and, yes, swans.

In González Martínez's autobiography, *La apacible locura* (Placid Madness,
1951), he soft-pedals suggestions that his poems marked the "end" of *modernismo*, something that it actually did not do. As we know, "movements" do not
begin or end that abruptly. The momentum of all that refinement and exquisite
beauty was so powerful that, like the swan, it sailed on for many years.

Here then, some of González Martínez's own comments on the reper-
cussions of his poem from *La apacible locura*.

———⊛———

Among the poems of that fourth book [*Los Senderos Ocultos*] was the sonnet
"Tuércele el Cuello al Cisne," that Pedro Henríquez Ureña had, upon my second arrival in Mexico City with the volume tucked under my arm, considered a conscious, intentional, literary manifesto, or as the synthesis of an
aesthetic doctrine. In truth, the poem was not written with a specific design
either for or against, but rather as a reaction against certain modernist

themes extracted from the opulent lyrical baggage of Rubén Darío — the Darío of *Prosas Profanas* [Profane Prose] and not the Darío of *Cantos de Vida y Esperanza* [Songs of Life and Hope]. Leaving aside the essence of the great Nicaraguan's poetry, there was prolonged in his imitators what we could call superficiality and performance. It is clear that his imitators lacked the grace, the exceptional virtuosity, and the enchanting personality of the model. Nor could Darío's followers achieve the lyric emotion perceptible in his work from the time of *Prosas Profanas*, even in poems in which technical agility and mastery of form seemed the one creative intent, much less, the lyricism — already accomplished, mature, and wise — of Rubén's poetry in *Cantos*. [. . .] Those elements within reach of imitators were theme — swans, pages, princesses; meter — already learned from France or old Spanish prosody; reliance on adjectives, which by constant repetition had lost efficacy and novelty; and lexicon in general — sterile for those who, lacking a fecund and renovating spirit, attempted to appropriate them.

My poem that takes the swan as a symbol of immanent grace and the owl as a paradigm of meditative contemplation that delves into the abysses of internal life was written in protest to that disquieting, though ephemeral, mode. Nothing against Darío, other than inevitable personal discrepancies; nothing against his fascinating and stimulating poetry. The poets who followed him, with strength to accept the stimulus and continue their own path without stumbling, had to be grateful for the initial upheaval that helped them find a way through the grayness of the *fin de siècle*. [. . .] All literary movements, all so-called schools, are like that. They begin with a vigorous personality who awakens interest and compels imitation. But of that apparently collective effort, of the group that marches in unison with the voice of command of the leader, creators with their own enterprise fall away. Of that initial impulse, there is left in the true artist what nourishes his temperament, modifies it without deforming it. Thus it was with the Italianism of Garcilaso and Boscán, the *conceptismo* of Quevedo, the *culturanismo* of Góngora, the romanticism of Germany and England, with its Spanish extension through Espronceda in his *Diablo Mundo*. And so it was with Darío's Spanish American *modernismo*, which lasted until it was vanquished by the Generation of '98 in Spain. What endures in these literary revolutions is not the presence of the model, but the open roads to fields of freedom. The servility of imitation leaves a path cluttered with failures. Those who are triumphant, on the other hand, frequently lose sight of the point of departure.

I felt — seizing upon the occasion of a wake in honor of Darío — obliged to clarify these points and make rectification. And as I rendered a fervent homage to the author of *Azul* and tried to make clear that my poem in no way was a condemnation of his poetry, a young critic, assuredly very intelligent and a very good poet, asserted that with my words I had "attempted to erase twenty years of Mexican literature."

Despite my best efforts, all too frequently I continue to be the murderer of swans and worshipper of owls, with a subsequent lack of critical focus on other aspects of my work. I realize that it is difficult to follow step-by-step a long and patient evolution. A brief oeuvre is receptive to being contained in a formula, but a labor of years and years, deeply modified by living although essentially maintaining a personal tone, suffers, whether for good or ill, the influence of the current hour. More than once I have wished to reconstruct the spiritual moment of many of my distant poems, but I have attempted the impossible. I cannot remember what I was like when I wrote such and such a poem. Everything changes and everything is renewed in art and in life. Even works of genius resist the attempt to be enclosed within a formula. Dante is not forever confined within the circles of his Inferno.

Every work of poetry is a story strewn with discoveries and experience. Critics tend to overlook the protean dynamism of creation and cling to their first discovery, seeking the easy way and closing their eyes to inevitable and obvious evolution. But the poet persists in his task, hoping that some day curiosity, interest, enthusiasm, or a serendipitous occasion will reveal that there was in his poems something previously unnoticed that broke the narrow mold in which his work had been imprisoned. The renewed renown of poets already classified and little read is explained by this unexpected reevaluation.

MSP: Whatever González Martínez may confess or deny regarding the centrality of his avian metaphors in turn-of-the-century Mexican literature, he does reveal that they were primary in his own thought when he gave the title *El hombre del buho* (Man of the Owl, 1944) to one of his revealing autobiographical works, and *La Muerte del cisne* (The Death of the Swan), to his

collection of poems published in 1915, some five years following the brou-
haha of his "cygnicide." We cannot doubt his rejection of the superficial
excesses of the snowy plumes of the swan that sees nothing around it but the
reflected beauty of its graceful movement across the blue mirror of the lake,
or his grateful adherence to the tenets of the wise, and at times mysterious,
nocturnal observer that surveys the landscape of poetry, sees beneath and
above its surface, and portrays its truth in his writing.

In *La apacible locura*, González Martínez further comments that he did
not intend the death of *all* swans, that there are swans that "deserve an
ignominious death, but others that deserve to live and continue to display the
divine mysteries of their white question marks against blue waters."

However innocent, however purposeful, González Martínez's poem
stands as a work that both defined and defused a literary movement, a rare
manifesto that shone an unflattering light upon a writing intending to
present itself as the highest expression of beauty.

Wring the Neck of the Swan

Let us wring the neck of the swan of beguiling plumage,
alabaster against the blue of the fountain;
it parades its grace, but has no feeling for
nature's soul, the voice of lake and mountain.

It flees from any form and all expression
that does not resonate with the latent cadence
of its sublimity . . . adoring life,
it wishes life to note its obeisance.

But regard the wise old owl, spreading its wings
above Olympus, leaving the lap of Athena
ending high in that tree its taciturn flight.

It lacks the grace of the swan, but its restless eye,
which can penetrate the darkness, interprets
the mysterious book of the nocturnal silence.

Translated by Margaret Sayers Peden

Octavio Paz

(1914 – 1998)

Translation: The Literary and the Literal

Before Octavio Paz's death in 1997, Carlos Fuentes wrote that Paz was "the greatest living poet of the Spanish language," adding, "the corpus of Paz's poetic creation has grown simultaneously in several directions. First, as an inner renewal of the Spanish language, then as an outward connection of our renewed language with that of the world."

Few critics would dispute Fuentes's assessment of Latin America's most recent, and Mexico's first, Nobel laureate. Paz's fame in the Spanish-speaking world, and in many parts of North America and Europe, can be appreciated only if we equate it to the celebrity we accord entertainers, politicians, and sports heroes. That a literary figure can enjoy such prominence, such universal recognition, demands of a North American a learning process in cultural attitudes. Poetry, and literature in general, is deeply embedded in Mexican and Latin American culture.

It is not strange or esoteric to be a poet. Latins agree that poets have things to tell us (though as Latins have no exclusive claim to beatitude, they do not always listen). Latin American nations traditionally reward their writers with diplomatic posts, and Paz served as Mexico's ambassador to India until he resigned to protest the events of the 1968 student uprisings in Mexico. The acts and words of poets do have import in Mexico.

People think of Paz primarily as a poet—much of his work is available in English translation in *Collected Poems, 1957–1987*—but it must be noted that he is also a brilliant essayist and critic. His writings in those fields are so important that he would be considered a major Mexican author had he never written a line of poetry. Among his more than thirty prose works, his monumental appraisal of the time, life, and work of Sor Juana Inés de la Cruz is a landmark: a reconsideration and revision of the history of *Nueva España*, that is, colonial Mexico; his reading of the biography of Sor Juana (a "reading" because factual information is extremely limited); and a penetrating analysis of Sor Juana's writings. At the time of the publication of the English version in 1988, John Kenneth Galbraith wrote, "No one uses language, and here history, so to enrich knowledge and enlarge imagination as does Octavio Paz."

There are, in addition, significant treatises on the philosophy of poetry, *Pears from the Elm Tree* and *The Bow and the Lyre*, commentaries on literary figures and movements, such as his empathetic studies of Marcel Duchamp and the Mexican Xavier Villaurrutia, and *The Labyrinth of Solitude*, which remains the single most informative, most insightful, most beautifully written book on *mexicanidad*—what it is to be Mexican. The last chapter, "The Dialectic of Solitude," goes beyond the specifically Mexican condition to set forth Paz's views on the reasons for contemporary man's sense of isolation and his hopes that man will be allowed to return to dream and myth.

"Translation: The Literary and the Literal," Paz's provocative commentary on the art of translation, is pertinent not merely to translators and to those editors who must deal with their problems, for translation lies at the core of questions about language itself, how humans express their thoughts and emotions, how they communicate among themselves, and how they relate to their reality.

Perhaps had he known her, Paz would have agreed with Celia Gilbert that the word *translated* is far more encompassing than we have defined it.

> The bereaved wore white. What was there to mourn?
>
> If the message was true: Summer-Land, flowers, sky.
> God's call, *Come home.*
>
> Not "Died." "Translated."
> — CELIA GILBERT, "Translated"

———❦———

Learning to speak is learning to translate; when the child asks his mother for the meaning of some word, what he is really asking is that she translate the new word into his vocabulary. Translation within a language is not, in this sense, essentially different from translation between two languages. The history of every nation repeats the child's experience: even the most isolated tribe must, at some time, confront the language of an alien people. The astonishment, rage, horror, or amused perplexity we feel in response to the sounds of a language we do not know soon becomes doubt over the one we speak. Language loses its universality and is revealed as a plurality of languages, all foreign and unintelligible to each other. In the past, translation dispelled that doubt: though there is no universal language, languages form a universal society. Once certain difficulties are overcome, all can know and understand each other. And they understand each other because in different languages men always say the same things. The universality of the spirit was the answer to the confusion of Babel: there are many languages, but meaning is one. Pascal found in the plurality of religions a proof of Christianity's truth; translation responded to the diversity of languages with the ideal of a universal intelligibility. Thus, translation was not only an extra proof but a guarantee of the unity of the human spirit.

The modern age destroyed that security. When he rediscovered the infinite variety of the temperaments and passions and beheld the spectacle of a multitude of customs and beliefs, man began to stop recognizing himself in other men. Until then, the savage had been an exception. It was necessary to suppress him by conversion or extermination, by baptism or the sword. But the savage who appeared in eighteenth-century salons was a new creature. Although he could speak his hosts' language perfectly, he embodied an undeniable foreignness. He was no longer the subject of conversion but rather of argument and criticism; the originality of his judgments, the simplicity of his customs, and even the violence of his passions were proof of the madness and vanity, if not the infamy, of those baptisms and conversions. Change of direction: the religious search for a universal identity was followed by an intellectual curiosity bent upon discovering differences which were no less universal. Foreignness ceased to be an aberration and became exemplary. This exemplary quality is paradoxical and revealing: the savage was the civilized man's nostalgia, his other self, his lost half. Translation reflected these changes: no longer did it tend to seek out the ultimate identity of man, but instead became the vehicle of his uniqueness. Its function had consisted of revealing similarities over differences; from now on, it would show that those differences were irreducible, whether describing the strangeness of the savage or of our neighbor.

Doctor Johnson expressed the new attitude very well. During a trip, he wrote: "A blade of grass is always a blade of grass, whether in one country or another . . . Men and women are my subjects of inquiry; let us see how these differ from those we have left behind." Doctor Johnson's sentence may be interpreted two ways, and both foreshadow the double path which the modern age was to take. The first alludes to the separation between man and nature, a separation which would become opposition and combat; mankind's new mission is not salvation but rather domination over nature. The second refers to the separation between men. The world is no longer one world, an indivisible whole; it is split into Nature and Culture, and Culture is divided into cultures. There are a great many languages and societies; each language is a vision of the world and each civilization is a world. The sun in an Aztec poem is different from the sun in an Egyptian hymn — no matter that they speak of the same star. For over two centuries, first the philosophers and historians and now the anthropologists and linguists have accumulated proofs of the irreducible differences between individuals, societies, and epochs. The great division, hardly less profound than the separation of Nature and Culture, is between primitive and civilized societies;

immediately, the variety and heterogeneity of civilizations is clear. Within each civilization the differences are reborn: the languages we use to communicate with each other also confine us in an invisible net of sounds and meanings, so that nations are prisoners of the languages they speak. Within each language the divisions are reproduced: historical periods, social classes, generations. As for relations between isolated individuals who belong to the same community, each one is walled up in his own self.

All this should have discouraged translators. But it has not; moving in a contradictory and complementary direction, they translate more and more. The reason for this paradox is that in a way, translation overcomes the differences between two languages; in another way, it reveals them more fully. Thanks to translation, we find that our neighbors speak and think in modes which are distinct from our own. In one extreme, the world appears to us as a heterogeneous collection; in another, as a superimposition of texts, each slightly distinguishable from the one preceding it: translations of translations of translations. Each text is unique and is, simultaneously, the translation of another text. No text is entirely original because language itself, in its essence, is already a translation: first, of the non-verbal world and then, because every sign and phrase is a translation of another sign and phrase. But this rationale may be inverted without losing validity: all texts are original because each translation is distinct. Each translation, up to a point, is an invention and so constitutes a unique text.

The discoveries of anthropology and linguistics do not condemn translation, but rather a certain naive idea of translation. That is, the literal translation which in Spanish is called, significantly, *servile*. I do not mean that literal translation is impossible, but that it is not translation. It is a device, generally composed of words strung together, which helps us to read the text in its original language. This is closer to the function of a dictionary than to that of translation, which is always a literary procedure. In all cases, not excluding those (such as scientific works) in which it is necessary to convey definition only, translation implies a transformation of the original. This transformation is nothing if not literary — it cannot be less. According to Roman Jakobson, all literary processes can be reduced to two modes of expression: metonymy and metaphor. And all translations utilize these modes. The original text never reappears in another language; that would be impossible. Nevertheless, it is always present because translation, without uttering the exact words of the original, either refers to it constantly or changes it into a verbal object which, although distinct, is a reproduction: metonymy or metaphor. These two forms, unlike explanatory or paraphrased translations, are rigorous and in no way detract from precision. The first is an indirect description and the second is a verbal equation.

The greatest condemnation of the possibility of translation has fallen upon poetry. A strange condemnation, when we remember that many of the best poems in every Western language are translations, and that many of those translations are the work of great poets. The critic and linguist Georges Mounin, in his recent book on translation (*Problèmes théorique de la traduction,* Gallimard, 1963), points out that it is generally, though begrudgingly, conceded that it *is* possible to translate the denotative meaning of a text; however, translation of connotative meaning is nearly unanimously held to be impossible. Poetry is a web of connotations, composed of echoes, reflections, and correlations between sound and meaning, and is, therefore, untranslatable. I confess that this idea is repugnant to me, not only because it goes against my idea of the universality of poetry, but also because it is based on an erroneous idea of the nature of translation. Many disagree with my ideas, and many modern poets declare that poetry is indeed untranslatable. Perhaps what motivates them is an immoderate love of verbal matter, or perhaps they have gotten tangled up in the trap of subjectivity. As Quevedo warns us, it is a fatal trap: "las aguas del abismo / donde me enamoraba de mi mismo . . ." ("the waters of the abyss / where I fell in love with myself . . ."). Unamuno presents an example of this verbal entrapment. In one of his lyrical-patriotic outbursts, he says:

> Avila, Málaga, Cáceres,
> Játiva, Mérida, Córdoba,
> Ciudad Rodrigo, Sepúlveda,
> Ubeda, Arévalo, Frómista,
> Zumárraga, Salamanca,
> Turéngano, Zaragoza,
> Lérida, Zamarramala,
> sois nombres de cuerpo entero,
> libres, propios, los de nomina,

el tuétano intraducible
de nuestra lengua española.

El tuétano intraducible de la lengua española ("the untranslatable marrow of
the Spanish tongue") is a bizarre metaphor (marrow and tongue?), but perfectly translatable because it refers to a universal experience. Scores of
poets have used this same rhetorical device, except that they have done so in
other languages. Their lists of words differ but the context, emotion, and significance are analogous. Moreover, it is curious that the untranslatable
essence of Spain should consist of a sequence of Roman, Arabic, Celtiberian,
and Basque names. Also curious is the fact that Unamuno translates the
name of the Catalan city Lleida into Spanish — Lérida. And the strangest
thing is that he cites this verse by Victor Hugo as the epigraph for his poem,
without realizing that by doing so he disproves the presumed untranslata-
bility of those names:

Et tout tremble, Irun, Coïmbre,
Santander, Almodovar
sitôt qu'on entend le timbre
des cymbals de Bivar.

In Spanish and French the meaning and emotion are the same. Since the
names themselves are not strictly translatable, Hugo limits himself to
repeating them in Spanish, without the slightest attempt to Frenchify them.
The repetition is effective because those words, stripped of all definite
meaning, become verbal bell-ringing, true *mantras*. They resonate through
the French text with even greater mystery than they do in the Spanish.
Translation is very difficult, no less so than writing texts which are more or
less original, but it is not impossible. Hugo and Unamuno show in their
poetry that connotative meanings can be preserved if the poet-translator
successfully reproduces the verbal situation, the poetic context in which
they are set. Wallace Stevens has given us a kind of archetypical formation of
such a setting in this admirable passage:

. . . . the hard hidalgo
Lives in the mountainous character of his speech;
And in that mountainous mirror Spain acquires

> The knowledge of Spain and of the hidalgo's hat —
> A seeming of the Spaniard, a style of life,
> The invention of a nation in a frase . . .

Language becomes the landscape and landscape, in turn, is an invention, the metaphor for a nation or an individual. In this verbal topography, everything is expressive and everything is translation: phrases are a mountain range and mountains are signs, ideograms of a civilization. But the play of verbal echoes and correspondences, aside from making us dizzy, conceals a marked danger. Surrounded by words on all sides, there comes a moment when we are caught off guard, alarmed at our strange situation of living among names and not things. The strangeness of having a name:

> Entre los juncos y la baja tarde
> qué raro que me llame Federico!

This experience, too, is universal: García Lorca would have felt the same strangeness whether his name had been Tom, Jean, or Chuang-Tzu. Losing one's name is like losing one's shadow; to be nothing more than a name is to be reduced to a shadow. To declare no relation between things and their names is doubly intolerable: either meaning then vanishes or things themselves disappear. A world made purely of meaning is as inhospitable as a world of things without meaning — without names. Language renders the world habitable. The sensation of perplexity at the strangeness of being called Federico or So Ji is instantly followed by the invention of another name — a name which is, in a sense, translation in the ancient manner: metaphor or metonymy which tells by not telling.

In the past few years there has been a tendency to minimize the eminently literary nature of translation, perhaps because of the imperialist attitude of linguistics. There is not nor can there be a science of translation, although it can and should be studied scientifically. In the same way that literature is a special function of language, translation is a special function of literature. And as for translation by machine? When those devices succeed in real *translation*, they will be performing a literary operation; they will do nothing less than what translators are doing now, and that is literature. Translation is a task in which the translator's initiative is the decisive factor (along with the essential linguistic erudition), whether we speak of a machine programmed by a man or a man surrounded by dictionaries. As further evidence of this, let us consider Arthur Waley's remark: "A French scholar wrote recently with regard to translators: 'Qu'ils s'effacent derrière les texts et ceux-ci, s'ils ont été vraiment compris, parleront d'eux-mêmes.' Except in the rather rare case of plain concrete statements such as 'The cat chases the mouse' there are seldom sentences that have exact word-to-word equivalents in another language. It becomes a question of choosing between various approximations . . . I have always found that it was I, not the texts, that had to do the talking." It would be difficult to add another word to that declaration.

In theory, only poets ought to translate; in practice, poets are rarely good translators. This is because they almost always use the foreign-language poem as a point of departure for their own poem. The good translator goes in the opposite direction: his goal is a poem which is analogous, although not identical, to the original. He moves away from it only to trace it more closely. The good translator of poetry is a translator who is also a poet, like Arthur Waley, or a poet who is also a good translator, like Nerval translating the first Faust. Other times, Nerval did *imitations*, which were admirable and really *originals*, of Goethe, Jean-Paul, and other German poets. An "imitation" is translation's twin sister: there is a resemblance, but it is important not to confuse them. They are like Justine and Juliette, the two sisters in de Sade's novels . . . The reason that many poets are incapable of translating poetry is not purely psychological, although egotism does play a part, but rather functional: poetic translation, as I intend to demonstrate, is an operation analogous to poetic creation. The only difference is that it unfolds in an inverse manner.

Each word contains a multitude of implicit meanings; as soon as a word is linked with others to constitute a phrase, one of those meanings is given life and becomes predominant. In prose, such meaning tends to be unequivocal while in poetry, as has been remarked so often, the multitude of meanings is perhaps the fundamental characteristic. The truth is that this characteristic is a general property of language. Poetry accentuates it, but it is manifested as well in common speech and even in prose, though in diluted form. (This factor confirms that prose, in the strict sense of the word, does not really exist: it is an ideal category of thought.) The critics have lingered over this disturbing feature of poetry, without perceiving that another equally fascinating detail is related to this type of mobility and indeterminateness of meaning: the immobility of signs. Now then, language is a system of mobile signs which are interchangeable to a certain extent: one word can be substituted for another and each sentence may speak for (or translate) another. To parody Peirce, one might say that the meaning of a word is always another word. To prove this, it is sufficient to remember that whenever we ask "What does that sentence mean?", we are answered with another sentence. So, we are hardly very deep into the field of poetry before words lose their mobility and interchangeability. The meanings of a poem are manifold and ever-changing; the words of that same poem are unique and irreplaceable. To change them would destroy the poem. Poetry, without ceasing to be language, is a step beyond language.

The poet, immersed in the movement of language, in its continuous flow, chooses a few words (or is chosen by them). Combining them, he constructs his poem: a verbal object made of irreplaceable and immovable signs. The translator's point of departure is not language in motion (the poet's raw material), but the fixed language of the poem. Congealed language which is, nevertheless, perfectly alive. His operation is the inverse of the poet's: it does not deal with the construction of mobile signs into an immobile text, but rather with dismantling the elements of the text, putting the signs back into circulation and returning them to language. Up to this point, the translator's activity resembles that of the reader and critic. Each reading is a translation and each critique is (or begins as) an interpretation. But reading is a translation within the same language and the critique is a free version (or, more exactly, a transposition) of the poem. To the critic, a poem is a point of departure for another text (his own), while the translator must compose, in another language and with different signs, a poem analogous to the original. Thus, the second stage of the translator's work is parallel to the poet's, with this essential difference: as he writes, the poet does not know how his poem will turn out; as he translates, the translator knows that he is obliged to reproduce the poem which he must keep always in sight. In its two stages, translation is parallel to poetic creation, although in an inverse manner. As a result, the translator is aware that his poem must reproduce the poem which has already been spoken, not by making a copy of it so much as a transmutation. As Valéry once masterfully defined it, poetic translation ideally consists of producing analogous effects by different means.

Translation and creation are twin operations. On the one hand, as demonstrated by Baudelaire and Pound, translation is often indistinguishable from creation. On the other hand, there is an incessant flow between the two, a continuous and mutual fertilization. The great creative periods of Western poetry, from its origin in Provence to modern times, have been preceded or accompanied by the interweaving of different poetic traditions. This interweaving sometimes takes the form of imitation and sometimes that of translation. From this point of view, the history of European poetry might be seen as a history of conjunctions: diverse traditions which form what is called Western literature (thereby omitting the Arab presence in Provençal lyric or that of haiku and Chinese poetry in modern poetry). Critics study "influences" but that is an ambiguous term; it makes more sense to consider Western literature as a unified whole in which the central characters are not national traditions (English, French, Portuguese, and German poetry), but rather styles and tendencies. No tendency or style has been national, not even "artistic nationalism." All styles have been trans-linguistic: Donne is closer to Quevedo than to Wordsworth; there is a clear affinity between Góngora and Marino while, on the other hand, nothing except language unites Góngora and the Arcipreste de Hita; the latter, in turn, seems at times to suggest Chaucer. Styles are collective and they pass from one language to another; literary works, all deeply rooted in their verbal ground, are unique . . . Unique but not isolated: each one is born and lives in relation to other works in different languages. In this way, neither the plurality of languages nor the singularity of works signifies irreconcilable heterogeneity or confusion. On the contrary, they form a world of related parts, contradictions and correspondences, unions and divisions.

In every period, European poets (and now also those from both Americas) write the same poem in different languages. Each one of these versions is also an original and distinct poem. Of course, they are not perfectly simultaneous, but we need draw back only slightly to realize that we are hearing a concert in which the musicians are composing a collective work without obeying any conductor or following any score. Improvisation is inseparable from translation and invention from imitation. At times, one of the musicians will launch into an inspired solo; in a little while the others follow him, not without introducing variations which change the original motif into something completely different. At the end of the last century, French poetry astounded and scandalized Europe with the solo begun by Baudelaire and finished by Mallarmé. The Spanish-American "modernist" poets were among the first to perceive this new music; imitating it, they made it their own, changing it and transmitting it to Spain, which, in turn, recreated it once more. A little later, English-speaking poets gave a similar performance, but with other instruments and a different tonality and tempo. Their version was more temperate and critical; Laforgue, and not Verlaine, occupied the central position. Laforgue's unique place in Anglo-American modernism helps explain the character of that movement, which was at once symbolist and anti-symbolist. Pound and Eliot followed Laforgue in introducing a critique of symbolism within symbolism itself, mocking what Pound called "funny symbolist trappings." This critical attitude soon prepared them to write poetry which was modern rather than "modernist," thus beginning (along with Wallace Stevens, William Carlos Williams, and others) a new solo: the solo of contemporary Anglo-American poetry.

Laforgue's fate in English and Spanish poetry is an example of the interdependence of creation and imitation, translation and original work. The French poet's influence on Eliot and Pound is well known, but few know of his influence on Spanish-American poets. In 1905, the Argentine Leopoldo Lugones, one of the greatest and least-studied poets of our language, published a book of poems, *Los crepúsculos del jardin*, in which several Laforguean features appeared for the first time in Spanish: irony, contrast between colloquial and literary language, and violent images of urban absurdity juxtaposed against nature, which had become a grotesque matron. Some of the poems in that book seemed to be written in one of those *dimanches bannis de L'Infini*, Sundays of the Spanish-American bourgeoisie at the end of the century. In 1909, Lugones published *Lunario Sentimental.* In spite of being an imitation of Laforgue, it was one of the most original books of its time and still may be read with amazement and delight. *Lunario Sentimental* had enormous influence over Spanish-American poets, but was most beneficial and stimulating to the Mexican López Velarde. In 1919, López Velarde published *Zozobra*, the central work of Spanish-American "post-modernism," that is, our own anti-symbolist symbolism. Two years before, Eliot had published *Prufrock and Other Observations.* In Boston, recently emerged from Harvard, a Protestant Laforgue; in Zacatecas, escaped from a seminary, a Catholic Laforgue. Eroticism, blasphemy, humor, and, as López Velarde said, an "intimate reactionary sadness." The Mexican poet died shortly afterward, in 1921 at the age of 33. His work ends where Eliot's begins . . . Boston and Zacatecas: the union of these two names makes us smile as if it were one of those incongruous associations which gave so much pleasure to Laforgue. Two poets write, at almost the same time, in different languages and without either one even suspecting the existence of the other, two different and equally *original* versions of some poems which had been written, several years before, by a third poet in another language.

Translated by Lynn Tuttle

Rosario Castellanos

(1925 – 1974)

Selections

Rosario Castellanos was born in Mexico City on May 25, 1925. Daughter of
a well-to-do family, she graduated with a degree in philosophy from the
Universidad Nacional Autónoma de México and took postgraduate courses
at the Universidad de Madrid. Castellanos's interests led immediately to
writing—her first book of poetry was published in 1948—and to work among
the Indians of the Chiapas region, where she had lived as a girl. From 1952 to
1961—with the exception of a year in 1956–57, during which, through the
auspices of the Rockefeller Foundation, she worked on her poetry—she held
various appointments in Chiapas, in institutes concerned with Indian issues.
She later worked as a press officer at the national university, where she also
taught literature courses.

Castellanos began her literary career as a poet, though she went on to
write novels, plays, and essays as well. As a poet she figures among the
Generation of the Fifties, but as such classifications are artificial, it should be
pointed out that she straddled the boundary between that group and the
movement known as *La Ruptura*, writers who broke all the molds.

Castellanos was an original. One must look back three centuries, to Sor
Juana Inés de la Cruz, to find a major woman writer in Mexico. And Rosario,
too, was a "rupturer." In *Album de familia*, *Sobre cultura feminina*, and a
collection of plays, *El eterno femenino*, one hears the stirrings of feminist

themes that anticipate the many women writers soon to follow: Elena Poniatowska, Margo Glantz, Silvia Molina, Angeles Mastretta, Carmen Boullosa, Sara Sefchovich, and Laura Esquivel, among others.

Again breaking molds, Castellanos returned to the setting of her early years to write about the marginalized Indians of that region. *Balún Canán*, *Oficio de tinieblas* (Book of Lamentations), and *Los nueve guardianes* (The Nine Guardians) form a trilogy that offers remarkable insight into the unexplored world of the Indians of Chiapas. In *Balún Canán*, she created an imaginary uprising of Chamula Indians in the 1920s, a fictional rebellion but one based on a historical event of 1867. Again Castellanos's work looks back to the earliest voices in Mexican literary history—this time to the writings of Bartolomé de las Casas and his defense of the New World Indian—and forward to Subcomandante Marcos and present-day upheavals in that southernmost state of Mexico.

In 1971 Castellanos was named Mexico's ambassador to Israel. She lived and served there until her life was tragically cut short by a freak accident with a defective electrical appliance, a serious loss to Mexico's literary community.

In the following section from *Mujer que sabe Latín* (Woman Who Knows Latin), Castellanos recounts her childhood romance with language and with the antecedents of language: sounds. We learn how that fascination rescued her from an unhappy reality and sustained her throughout a lifetime: a lifeline that may be the rationale for much of writing and reading.

Early Writings

I don't see the discovery of a literary vocation as a conscious act through which a previously hidden truth is suddenly revealed, remaining thereafter open to corroboration, subject to the laws of development, always seeking realization.

No: I see the discovery of a literary vocation as a phenomenon that exists on a much more profound and more elemental level of human experience: at the depths where instinct, blindly yet effectively, finds a response to sudden emergency, to extreme danger, matters of life and death in which a person wagers everything on a single card . . . and wins.

I'm not talking about myself, not yet. I'm thinking of the narrator of *Remembrance of Things Past*, who, as an awestruck, curious child, witnesses his family's preparations for a formal dinner, which, naturally, he may not attend because those rituals are inappropriate for someone his age.

The prohibition disappoints him, of course. But what causes him nearly unbearable anguish is the certainty that his mother will not leave her place at the table in order to go upstairs to give him his customary good-night kiss.

And yet, against all expectations of logic and habit, the narrator impatiently awaits what could only be a miracle. In order to force the miracle to happen, he scribbles a little message, a peremptory, "Come here!" which a servant carries to its recipient but to which he receives no reply, much less the fulfillment of his request.

Nevertheless, the narrator — simply by virtue of having written that note — feels the tension that was consuming him diminish, as if the act of writing had worked on him (although not on the external situation) like a balm. Something mysterious has occurred: a liberating change.

How could one resist repeating the attempt to evoke this inexplicable occurrence once more? And so the narrator does. Every time the world closes in on him, every time the abyss yawns, every time the sky tumbles, there it is, right on his lips: the word, the incantation, which, once pronounced, restores peace to his spirit and order to chaos, two related and mutually complementary realities.

But, as in the Cernuda poem, I, at the same age as the narrator of *Remembrance of Things Past*, "didn't speak words." I inhabited a realm before language, one of pure sounds that I later learned could be harmonized into sequences and correspondences. It was then that I learned to recite the alphabet.

What can cure vertigo? Vowels. Yes, as I pronounced them, my effort slowed their speed — like a carousel whose motor is beginning to wind down — until whatever was making me dizzy, confusing me, grew quiet, as though inviting me to climb aboard. Because the mechanism was about to start up again, and we'd be better off spinning along with it than watching from afar.

I hop on the carousel — with the incantation melting in my mouth — and each time the momentum makes it whirl out of orbit, I give it rhythm with the mere enunciation, in sequence, of the *a*, the *e*, the *i*, the *o*, the *u*. And the rhythm is so even and so gentle that it reminds me of the breathing of a sleeping child. Yes, I've fallen asleep, and I dream that my brother isn't dead, that my parents are with me, that the house is small, without a single empty space where ghosts, bats, or witches might lurk.

A house my own size . . . not this vastness that needs to be filled with consonants. Twenty-two of them in my language, though there aren't enough of them and I can't seem to invent more. Oh well, I'll just have to repeat some of them: the most melodious ones, the most emphatic, the most definitive. There are no rules. Every night I choose, using my own judgment and the requirements that must be satisfied. While I carry out this task (so much like that of the boy Agustín spied on the beach, trying to empty the sea with a little bowl), I'm no longer the child death shunted aside in favor of the other one, the better one, my brother. I'm not the girl left alone by her parents to diligently sob away her grief. I'm not that pitiful figure who wanders along deserted hallways and doesn't go to school or out walking or anywhere at all. No. I'm almost a person. I have the right to exist, to stand before others, to walk into a classroom, stride up to the blackboard and subtract fractions, climb onto a podium draped with tissue paper and recite these verses:

> What's the matter?
> Where can poor Perlín be hiding?
> Granny runs up and down,
> Searching all the corners of the house.

Perlín is a cat. The rest is anecdote . . . and music. Couldn't it be imitated? Well, imitation is still too overwhelming an enterprise for my limited resources. But copying, on the other hand . . . Not an exact copy, of course. I'm not ready for that, either. But an acceptable approximation. Let's begin by saying *Perrín* instead of *Perlín*. But if we say *Perrín*, we conjure up a domestic animal that's the opposite of a cat: its natural enemy, the dog, or *perro*. From there on in, the story will take another route, develop differently, lead to a different conclusion.

On second thought, the dog doesn't convince me at all. The one I once knew was too lively, too restless, too difficult to manage. I'll choose a stuffed dog, instead. Or better yet: an imaginary dog. One that's never had density, volume, weight, or bark. A dog of my own invention. His name is Rin Tin Tin.

The sound of these syllables evokes something familiar in me. Finally I make the connection: Yes, Rin Tin Tin is the hero of a thousand adventures boisterously announced by the only illustrated children's publication of the day: *Paquín*. The couplet resounds with the fatalism of inevitability:

> I like to read *Paquín*
> 'cause it stars Rin Tin Tin.

I write it on the pages of a school notebook, and the moment I read it, I realize that these two lines engendered in the pit of my belly have just severed their umbilical cord, freed themselves from me, and are now staring me in the face: autonomous, absolutely independent, and even more remarkable, like strangers.

I don't recognize them as objects that once belonged to me, but rather as objects that are there, prodding me to acquire a greater, more perfect level of existence: a public existence.

They refuse to stay on the pages of that notebook where only my eyes can read them, aspiring instead to relocate somewhere else, somewhere they'll be exposed to the gaze of others. And so I obey, copying the lines on good stationery, placing that in an envelope and mailing it to the children's magazine, which has a page devoted to its readers' spontaneous contributions. There, once the necessary time has elapsed, I will marvel at those two lines — now set in print and repeated infinitely in an infinite number of copies — with my name at the bottom. I am the author of this thing that others read, talk about, of this thing they appropriate and claim for themselves and recite in their own way and interpret however they like. I can't do anything to stop it, to change it. I am disconnected from them, separated forever from what I once harbored within me as one harbors — no, I refuse to employ the conventional simile — a child, to which the written work is always compared. Besides, I don't have the slightest notion of what maternity is like. But, on the other hand, I do understand what illness is. We agree, then, that I harbored the couplet within me like an illness.

And now I'm cured. But still exposed to many aches and pains. It's no longer a dog that's barking all around me, asking me to name him. It's I who want to see myself on display in order to know myself, to recognize myself. But what's my name? Whom do I resemble? From whom do I differ? With pen in hand, I begin a quest that offers respite in that it's made some discoveries, but it remains unfinished.

If "Poetry, You're Not," Then What Are You?

How to justify a book? It's simpler to write another one and leave it to the critics to make the confusing seem explicit, the vague seem precise, the erratic seem systematic, and the arbitrary seem substantial. But when, as in my case, all of one's books of poetry are combined into one volume that, when opened, reveals a first verse that affirms, "*The world moans, sterile as a mushroom*," there remains no choice but to offer a hurried explanation. For, as observers pointed out to me at the time, the mushroom is the antithesis of sterility, proliferating, in fact, in shameless abundance and almost effortlessly. And, in truth, what I had meant to say was that the world came about as spontaneously as a mushroom, that it didn't spring forth from some divine plan and wasn't the result of the internal laws of matter or the *conditio sine qua non* for the development of the human drama. That the world was, in short, a perfect example of serendipity.

Why, then, didn't I say what I meant? Simply because I didn't accept the task. And I should add that inertia, even more than conviction, led me to wave, like a banner of my faith, the flag of a Latin America that was more rhetorical than real. I was no optimist in those days, but pessimism struck me as a wrongheaded, private attitude, the product of childhood trauma and a troubled adolescence. I didn't have the slightest idea of what "the continent's death throes" meant, either, but I had given so little thought to the phrase that it didn't capsize along with all my other beliefs following a serious crisis of values that left me stranded in the midst of the most turbulent Cartesian waters.

But (I realize now) I have turned the book's cover without stopping to

reflect on it. The title — *If Poetry, You're Not* — deserves a paragraph all to itself.
A rebellion, after all this time, against the Spanish romanticism that Bécquer
embodied so well? We may be anachronistic, but we're not *that* anachronistic!
A contradiction of Rubén Darío's more recent affirmation that one cannot *be*
without being Romantic? No, not that, either. What happened is that I made
a very slow transition from the most hermetic subjectivity to the disturbing
discovery of the existence of the Other, and finally, to the breaking of the
couple-mold in order to assimilate into the social realm, which is where the
poet defines, comprehends, and expresses himself. The *zoon politikon* cannot
achieve that realm unless there is a minimum number of three. Even in the
Gospel, Christ assures us that wherever two or more gather in His name, the
divine spirit will come to rescue them from their solitude.

Are we talking about a French ménage à trois, then? A spicy vaudeville
act? Nothing could be further from my intention. For the time being, the
link among the components doesn't necessarily have to be amorous. But if it
is, it's because I've always thought of love as one of the instruments of catastrophe. Not because it can't achieve plenitude or permanence. That's the
least of it. The crux of it is that, like what happened to Saint Paul, love pulls
the scales from our eyes and we see ourselves as we are: needy, petty, cow-
ardly. Careful not to risk all through surrender or to commit ourselves by
accepting what's offered. Love is no consolation, as Simone Weil affirmed.
And, as she added ominously, it's light. That light from which the soul
retreats in order to avoid seeing its depths illuminated, beckoning us to
plunge in, to be annihilated, and then? . . . The promise is unclear. What follows could be nothingness, inconceivable to our intelligence although
attractive to that part of us that longs for an absolute end to suffering. Or,
perhaps to be born on another plane of existence, marvelously serene, that
paradise that Jorge Guillén condenses into a singe verse: "Where love is not
anguish."

And so it seems that, after so much scurrying about, in the end I'm just a
poetess (or "poetass," to use Mejía Sánchez's term) who (also!) writes about
love. Be still, O shades of Delmira Agustini, Juana de Ibarbourou, and
Alfonsina Storni! It's not exactly the same thing. I wouldn't want to resign
myself to believing it's the same thing. It's true that I read these poets with
a true apprentice's diligence. It's true that I admired the first one's lush

imagery and the third's ironic smile, as well as the direct and indirect suicidal impulse they both shared. It's true that I learned from the second one that all her work was alien to me. But my problem came from other sources and therefore demanded other solutions.

When the moment to discover a vocation arrived, I learned that mine was to understand. Until then, I had unconsciously identified that urgency with writing. Whatever came out. And what came out were consonantal hendecasyllables. A pair of quatrains and a pair of couplets. Sonnets. And writing them relieved my anguish as if, for a single instant, I had liberated myself from chaos. Order reigned. A ridiculous kind of order, perhaps, and certainly a temporary one, but order nonetheless.

Someone informed me that what I was doing was called literature. Later I found out that there was a department at the university where its history and practice were studied. I went to enroll, if only to convince myself that the list of dates and names, the cataloging of styles, and the analysis of techniques didn't help me to understand it one bit. That not only did the formal study of literature lack answers to the big questions but also that the big questions weren't even being asked. Questions like: Why? For what purpose? How? I'm referring, of course, to everything.

My guardian angel on duty at the time pointed out that right next door to the literature classes, classes in philosophy were being offered. And that's where it happened. I'm referring, of course, to everything.

I changed classrooms. "Happy, unnoticed, and confident," I began to receive instruction in the pre-Socratic philosophers. Who, if memory serves me, wrote poems. Parmenides and Heraclitus flesh out their concept of the world with the image. As does Plato, although he *does* struggle to draw a dividing line between the two ways of knowing, and he throws poets out of his Republic because they carry an undesirable trace of dissoluteness. Then along comes Aristotle, and the separation between philosophy and letters is complete.

When I realized that philosophical language was inaccessible to me and that the only concepts within my reach were disguised as metaphors, it was already too late. Not only was I about to finish my degree, but I no longer wrote hendecasyllables or consonants or sonnets. I was something else. Amphibious. Ambiguous. And, like the cross of different species, sterile.

The evidence? Countless destroyed manuscripts and the first two poems of the collection we were discussing earlier: *Notes for a Declaration of Faith* and *The Trajectory of Dust* (which, incidentally, were written in a chronological order different from the one in which they appear in the book. One can't tell. There's so little progression from one text to another).

The unpardonable sin of both poems is the abstract vocabulary I used in them. It became essential for me to supplement it with another, more accessible vocabulary in which the themes could take on a palpable consistency.

In order to escape from this dead-end street, I found no better solution than to provide myself with a model, an example. And then, to copy it as laboriously and as faithfully as possible. I chose Gabriela Mistral, the Gabriela of "Matter," of the "Creatures," and of "Messages." Gabriela, the reader of the Bible. Reading to which I applied myself as well, naturally. The fine shadow of such fine trees (and of their foliage) falls on the pages of *The Sterile Vigil.*

An unfortunate title that allowed my friends to invent jokes: sterile or *hys*-teri-cal? I was single, but not by choice, and the drama of that rejection of the most obvious aspects of my femininity was genuine. But who would have ever guessed, if it was obscured by such a dense leaf storm? I had arrived at the same conclusion as the sculptor: the statue is what's left after all the excess rock is chipped away.

My watchword, therefore, became simplicity. I proceed, much more lightly, to *The World's Ransom*. And, almost weightless, I astound myself with *The Joyful Mysteries* and *The Splendor of Being.*

But, as Saint Augustine said, the heart is what weighs us down. Like the weight that throws a poem off balance. A *Total Eclipse*, yes, but a brief one. Our suffering is so great that it spills from the vessel of our body in search of more ample containers. It finds paradigmatic figures in tradition. Dido, who elevates the triviality of the situation (is there anything more trivial than a deceived woman and a faithless man?) to the majestic realm where the wisdom of the ages resounds.

Dido's Lament, besides being an individual mishap, is the convergence of two readings: Virgil and St. John Perse. One gives me the substance and the other the form. And then comes the privileged moment of smooth coupling and the birth of the poem.

The poem, which loomed immediately before me like an obstacle. I was so afraid to rewrite it! I was so afraid not to! Until, finally, I decided to ignore it. And to start from scratch with *Word for Word*.

Surrounded by so many echoes, I begin to recognize that of my own voice. Yes, I'm the one who wrote *The Toad's Soirée*, as well as *The Foreigner's Monolgoue* and *The Soothsayer's Tale*. Three threads to follow: humor, serious meditation, contact with our historical and carnal roots. And all of it bathed in the *Ashen Light* of death, which makes all matter memorable.

As I've said, I pause here because I don't like to admit to stagnation. Some strong outside force must come along and shake me up, making me change perspective, renew my style, opening the door to new themes, new words.

Many of them are vulgar, coarse. What can I do? They're the ones I need in order to say what must be said. Nothing too important or transcendent. A few glimpses of the organization of the world, some coordinates for me to locate myself within it, the mechanism of my relationship with other beings. Neither sublime nor tragic. A little bit ridiculous, maybe.

One has to laugh, after all. And laughter, as we know, is the first evidence of freedom. And I feel so free that I initiate a "Dialogue with the Most Honest of Men," that is, with other writers. On a first-name basis. Disrespect on my part? A lack of culture, if by culture we mean what Ortega defined as a sense of rank? Perhaps. But let's give ourselves the benefit of the doubt. And let's give the *reader-accomplice* the task of developing a different hypothesis, different interpretations.

The Agony of Choosing

The game (a party game? a game of wits? or of pure leisure?) that consists of asking a supposed literary dilettante or professional which ten books he would take with him in the hypothetical situation of going off to a desert island has only one reasonable response: a copy of the *The Compleat Castaway* would be enough. Someone must have written such a book at one time or another because it's impossible to imagine a world without it. Everything else would be superfluous.

Besides, no one ever knowingly goes off to a desert island. Just as no one went off to the Hundred Years' War, either, until a century later some historian gave it that name. Nevertheless, there are certain situations when we must choose from among those many friends we acquire through the years, those to whom we feel close or by whom we feel abandoned, as well as those we return to at special moments of happiness or dark moments of tears, we must choose. Because it's never possible to take one's entire library along, no matter how humble it may be.

Let's imagine ourselves at one of those moments, since it's not too difficult to imagine and since our present circumstances can help us to do so. How tempting it would be to choose the complete works of Proust, of Thomas Mann (whose complete letters have just been published and in which, despite their deep intimacy, he never loses his nobility), of Tolstoy! And why not, if we owe them so many revelations, so many pleasures that grow through recollection and rereading, so many discoveries that have helped us, not only to understand but, more fundamentally, to live? Well, for the simple reason that these gentlemen are worth their weight and transporting them would be unaffordable.

Let's eliminate, then, and for the same reasons, *The Human Comedy*, all of Pérez Galdós's novels, the Galsworthy sagas that lately, by one of those unpredictable whims of fate, have become fashionable again, and let's proceed to narrow the field.

The titles we've eliminated won't be hard to find anywhere we may be going. If our nostalgia becomes unbearable, we can find a copy of *Buddenbrooks* — and problem solved!

But our nostalgia won't be entirely literary. We'll feel nostalgia for the landscape to which our eyes have become accustomed ever since we were born. Nostalgia for particular modes of expression and behavior. For formulas, thanks to which we have established, delimited, expanded, or suspended our human relationships. It will be, in short, nostalgia for a lifestyle we have abandoned, albeit momentarily, in order to acquire, or at least rehearse, another.

Translated by Andrea Labinger

Emilio Carballido

(b. 1925)

Some Thoughts on Dramatic Composition

There is a saying that goes "Como México no hay dos" —there is only one Mexico; more literally, like Mexico there aren't two. These words can just as appropriately be applied to Emilio Carballido because there is no other like him.

As an author Carballido is primarily a playwright, though he has also written novels, short stories, and criticism. He is a pure man of the theater: author, teacher, administrator, mentor, director, and general promoter, always surrounded by aspiring actors and writers, always an inspiration to students, and forever Carballido, inimitable, the most Mexican of Mexican playwrights.

It is doubtful that anyone has the correct tally of Carballido's creations, the long, long lists of published and performed works. Mexicans have the tradition of installing plaques in theaters to mark the longest-running plays. Many of these bear Carballido's name. Mexicans also generously reward their literary stars with symposia, certificates, and celebrations, the most recent of which, in Carballido's case, was held in May 2005 in the Palacio de Bellas Artes in Mexico City, celebrating his eightieth birthday.

Carballido changed the course of Mexican theater. While he contributed a number of plays to the body of Mexican neorealistic/costumbristic plays, he raised Mexican theater above the traditionally limited level of that genre by introducing music, humor, poetry, formal innovation, and his own unique blend of realism and fantasy into post-forties Latin American theater. His plays have been presented around the globe, and his tales of travels in Russian Aeroflots and quixotic adventures in world capitals deserve a book of their own, illustrated, of course, by his amusing drawings of a feline alter ego that shares his travels and his dreams.

Carballido has an abiding interest in philosophical and metaphysical questions and in his writing repeatedly probes the eternal questions of the meaning of man's existence. Yet for all its seriousness, his writing is marked by an affectionate, puckish, and cathartic humor. That may be his greatest gift, that combination of deep message and high entertainment, if it is not his fusion of reality with flights of imagination—perhaps his own theatrical brand of magical realism.

The remarks that follow are not typical of those often heard at a speaker's acceptance into the vaunted Mexican Academy of Arts. They *are* Carballido.

———— 🐚 ————

We authors are frequently pressured to comment on our writing . . . by journalists when we are interviewed, by critics in exchanges about our work. They ask us to give an account of and rationale for our procedures when writing: the way in which our ideas are conceived, the relation between fiction and reality in what we write, the whole structure of the loom on which we weave our fantasies. And we answer as if we knew what it is we do, humbly offering the account and rationale they ask for, even if it isn't true — like children responding to grown-ups when they are afraid of being punished.

We are reluctant to explain something that we seldom pause to explain to ourselves: that writing literature is only partially rational, and that there is a give and a take in the resources we call on, and that this, too, is not easy to explain.

A story presents itself as a journey that must be undertaken: there is an opportune moment to begin and another to close, the parade of happenings that have marched past before us. But please keep in mind that reality has no beginning or end; it is infinite, and the author must choose the opportune moment in which events are ready to begin that parade, weave together the conflicts encountered along the way, and progress to the point at which the threads must be cut. Just as in a car moving at great speed, the driver's — the author's — decisions are instantaneous, instinctive, we might even say irrational, because one cannot reason while moving at dramatic speeds.

The truth about the process of composing a play is not that it is irrational, but that it is conceived and executed on a level in which the irrational mind fires much more rapidly than the rational. A scene is resolved only with instinct: a curtain falls when it must, a clever reply, an on-the-mark speech, are not the work of lucid thought but of that cluster of happenings in the drama in which events link together in a way that works for the characters. The writer contemplates and reports what is happening. In fantasy an independent world is created whose laws one learns and follows as they occur; felicitous events or catastrophes are independent of what the writer might wish. If it occurs to us to manipulate them or run roughshod over them, according to our reason or our will, they will be seriously harmed.

I think that being a writer must be something like being a medium: spirits come, speak through someone's mouth, say things that person did not know, behave independently from the person they inhabit, and leave when they royally please. They also come whenever they please, and are not necessarily well behaved.

And so it is with plays: they can even appear in dreams. I always counsel students in my workshops to keep a notebook nearby in which they can jot down their dreams as soon as they wake. There are some, especially, those that Jung calls "numinous," that contain entire stories, or at least the fertile seeds of a work begging to be written. I confess that dreams are a principal source of much of my work.

This method, of course, was invented by the Surrealists. The thinking of this artistic school is one of great coherence and offers highly useful avenues by which to penetrate the darkest zones of our beings, explore them, and from them extract valuable materials that, in passing, will also enrich our lives. If we write down our dreams at the very moment they are developing, we will not forget them, and we already know how useful they are for self-knowledge.

Another bit of advice to any who want to write: keep a diary of your life and thoughts. Rereading such a notebook tells us much about our own situation; it is a means of knowing oneself, for memory knows very well where the pen has lied. It is also a way to keep the days from fleeting by so irretrievably and, in the end, a very satisfying trail left on paper.

Something more to consider in regard to keeping a diary: The person who wants to learn to express himself through the written word must practice writing with some consistency and must learn to enjoy it. If you do not enjoy putting down your ideas, you have no chance of surviving a literary career: the best prize for writing is to write. And the pleasures of that practice are also learned.

All these things are connected: the knowledge of who we are cannot be separated from the act of writing (or of art in general). The person who does not know himself or delve deeply into his being, how can he intuit others? When we say that someone is "superficial," it seems to me to be a good definition of a person who is afraid to look into himself, who lives from borrowed prejudices and ready-made ideas, who is incapable of discovering, inventing, and guiding his own life.

By that I mean that he who does not try to explore himself to the deepest level (and that is not easy to do) is ill equipped to attempt to penetrate the complexity of his fellow beings. I advise my students to read their Freud and their Jung; I believe that they are more useful than any treatise on dramatic composition.

We have many treatises on dramatic writing, beginning with the *Poetics* of Aristotle, and the student may go to them when looking for a formula for what he must do. We must remember that all good treatises are a commentary on work already done, the procedures of how it was done. They are not formulas for inventing new works. These will be born by proposing our own laws, and those laws must be discovered and obeyed.

A writer cannot simultaneously be his own critic and be thinking, "What genre, what school will what I'm writing be classified under?" Theory is something one applies in general; creation is highly individual.

By that do I mean that the author must be ignorant of theory? Not at all. I believe he must review many theories and accept the sanest, along with those that are applicable for judging his own work — *after it has been written.*

The critique begins afterward. And it must begin afterward because the author who drools with adoration over his own work and asks the mirror, "Who is the fairest author of all?" is not a pretty sight. We know what the answer will be, and the result is attacks of fiendish envy when there is someone who, like Snow White, is just a little better author, or simply more acclaimed. Competition in art tends to damage talents. What is in sports a method of measuring excellence, is in art a fallacy. One good work is as good and as valuable as another good work, and there are not that many levels of quality. Worse is that the true weight and importance of artistic products is ascertained only with the passing of time; authors will learn in the next world whether these things continue to interest them.

The crafting of works is something we must distinguish from its ineffable essence: artistry. A good craftsman learns, refines, polishes. The art comes gratis, and it is not easy to express without good craftsmanship. If we want to keep the phoenix in our house, we must construct a cage in which it is comfortable, and happy. Of course, if we make the cage badly, the phoenix will burn in its own fire and consume us along with it — except that *we* will not be reborn.

And what about *engagé* theater, theater committed to social and political causes? Drama that distributes messages with both hands and tells us how to behave in society in order to better it and when to throw ourselves into the struggle? I believe it is the *citizen*, not the author, who must be committed. The citizen who also happens to write and who is the flesh and blood abode of the author. It is impossible to write against what we believe and what we are. We express our own vital creed. Sartre was an honorable man who wrote with deep ethical conviction; he dared write "Les main sales" [variously translated as "Crime passionel," "The Red Gloves," and "Dirty Hands"] though the entire Communist Party writhed with rage. Citizen Sartre was one of the best minds of the century and one of the most honorable and profound individuals.

Messages were more difficult for Brecht. He wanted to be an orthodox communist; in truth, he was an exceptional lyric and dramatic poet, and then his works betrayed him. He wrote *Mother Courage* three times: we were meant to be critical of Ana, the trafficker in war, and yet the reader, the audience, sympathized with her, suffered with her, and loved her. "Mann ist mann" [Man Equals Man] is unequivocal, but we all despise armies . . . or almost all of us. Citizen Brecht was a true *pícaro*, a rogue from the Golden Age, and a minister's son. He invented a marvelous theater that returned to the recourses of medieval and Renaissance genres, but he did not do well as a "committed" author. If one believes in a cause, the story will emerge of its own; but if one selects a social theme, drags a plot out by the feet to contain it, it is a good bet that the work may say the opposite of what we want it to say. Because one's writing comes from the depths of one's being, not from the will, or from an opportunistic, journalistic proposition.

There are many theories about drama. If we review them, we find that several coincide at basic points. Just as Aldous Huxley summed up the thought of a number of religions in *The Perennial Philosophy*, expounding on their coinciding points, it would be feasible to join together the convergent points of various poetics in a kind of "Eternal Poetics." And there we would undoubtedly find Aristotle, Lessing, Lope de Vega, and a bit of Durrenmat and T. S. Eliot.

It is to the author's benefit to review those texts, to find there, as in a mirror, "This is what I am doing." Which is not the same as "This is what I should do." The bad part about studying theories before writing is that the author may take them seriously and try to follow them. Nothing less advisable. Always remember the story of the centipede Gustav Meyrink tells in "The Curse of the Toad."

What to do then, if we want a personal guide for our dramaturgy? How to do better what we do? How to write meaningful works, accessible, yet universal. For young writers, I suggest several recipes that are not overly demanding.

First: write family portraits, about domestic crises you have personally witnessed. One advantage is that your relatives will either be furious with you, because they are about them, or they will love them, because they are about them. The family portrait helps us put distance and objectivity into events that are part of ourselves.

Practice exercises in listening. This I call "spy-work." I carry a little notebook and write down what my ears pick up in the café, at school, in my own home. This method requires some stealth, and a touch of hypocrisy. You jot down what you hear but with particular attention to *how* it is being said — the words, not the meaning. If the person(s) you are spying on realize what is happening, you may run into a little trouble, of course, but that is how you learn that dramaturgy has its risks.

From rough transcription, it is necessary to pass to elaboration. Only rarely do people speak with literary grace, with polish and euphony. This photographic retouching is a literary labor, slower than pure dramatic composition, and more difficult to perfect. There are many effective dramas that effortlessly please the public; they play well, they are interesting, intelligent . . . but when read, they turn out not to be art, only half-baked craftsmanship. The way people speak gives us models to imitate; in the works of the Golden Age we see clearly the different ways of speaking among peasants, fools, caballeros, and scholars. All expressed in beautiful poetry! That is a model to consider and compare with dialogue taken directly from real subjects.

The writer must select and polish. Drama is a literary art, and often its practitioners forget that point. I counsel students to practice classical verse, with meter and rhyme. The difficulty of finding music and harmony in words is evident in the laws of music, rhyme, and meter. I do not want poetry, merely polished, well-made verses that lend grace, ear, and craft to the writer's words. Free verse is more difficult, and often poets confuse terrible prose divided into long and short lines with poetry. One must sharpen one's quill and attempt to make the dialogue something beautiful.

Constant practice. The only way to become a writer is to write. The person who cannot find pleasure in editing page after page after page would be better off not writing. Period. I know people who have longed to be writers but are loath to do the writing to earn that title. Naturally, they are not good authors.

I do not know what more I can say about this calling. We try to make well-constructed cages for the phoenix, and for other fabled birds, but our true goal is that when we have finished, the birds will fly free. We want to populate stages with living beings, free and meaningful. Trying to achieve that consumes our lives. Our heirs will know whether we met with success.

Translated by Margaret Sayers Peden

Carlos Fuentes

(b. 1928)

Decalogue for a Young Writer

Carlos Fuentes. Ambassador extraordinaire. For Mexico. For Mexican literature. Fuentes is the son of diplomats and was himself Mexico's ambassador to France from 1975 to 1977. It is often suggested that had he not been born in Panama City, he would by now have been president of Mexico.

As a writer, Fuentes stands as a monolith in Mexico's literature: her greatest innovator, her most brilliant cultural and social analyst, her most visible representative abroad. He is one of the standard quartet of novelists— the others being Gabriel García Márquez, Julio Cortázar, and Mario Vargas Llosa—who personify the Latin American Boom, a phenomenon of literary creation and disruption.

Fuentes has won major prizes and taught in universities across three continents. Eloquent, witty, self-assured, and gifted with a penetrating mind, he has earned his place in the pantheon of Latin America's great writers. He has been quoted as saying that Spanish "is the language that with the greatest eloquence and beauty offers the broadest spectrum of the human soul." He also once told a translator that English is supposed to be the most "malleable language," so obviously it should not be difficult to recreate his novels and short stories in English. He explained to an interviewer who, after listening to a lecture Fuentes gave in flawless English, asked why he doesn't write in English. "I dream, count, curse, and make love in Spanish," he replied. "Therefore, I write in Spanish."

Like many Mexican writers before him, Fuentes has consistently explored the theme of *Mexicanidad*, the question of identity that has haunted Mexican intellectuals since the time of the Conquest. From the union between Cortéz and the Malinche was born the first Mexican mestizo, the bastard child of an Indian woman who gave herself to a conquering white god. In *Todos los gatos son pardos* (All Cats Are Gray) Fuentes explores the many facets of that symbolic betrayal.

In an interview on National Public Radio, Fuentes commented, "You have an absolute freedom in Mexican writing today, in which you don't necessarily have to deal with the Mexican identity. You know why? Because we *have* an identity. We know who we are. We know what it means to be a Mexican." And one might interject that this is in large part due to Fuentes himself. "Now the problem is to discover difference—not identity but difference: sexual difference, religious difference, political difference, moral differences, esthetic differences. . . ."

In his hundreds of lectures and scores of university courses, Fuentes has often been asked for advice and insights on writing. In "Decalogue for a Young Writer," he refines and condenses those views. That these commandments have been well tested may be seen in major novels such as *Where the Air Is Clear*, *The Death of Artemio Cruz*, *Terra Nostra*, *The Old Gringo*, *A Change of Skin*, and *The Days of Laura Díaz*.

COMMANDMENT NUMBER ONE:
DISCIPLINE

Books do not write themselves. Neither are they cooked in committee. To write is a solitary act, sometimes a frightening one. It is like entering a tunnel without knowing if there will be a light at the end, even if there will be an end at all.

I remember having spent many weekends, as a very young man, in the Mexican tropical town of Cuernavaca with the writer Alfonso Reyes, whom

Borges called the greatest prose writer in the Spanish language during the twentieth century. Reyes was nearly seventy, I was seventeen, and sometimes I came in from a *parranda* at five in the morning and saw the light in Reyes's study shining and Don Alfonso himself bent over his writing table like a magical shoemaker gnome.

He calmed my astonishment — let's say my envy, my desire to emulate him — with a sentence by Goethe, another early riser. "The writer must take the cream off the top of the day." So that after writing from five to eight, Goethe could go on to spend the day collecting stones, inventing a theory of light, counseling the court at Weimar, and chasing after chambermaids.

In any case, Alfonso Reyes taught me that discipline is the daily name of creation, and Oscar Wilde that literary talent is 10 percent inspiration and 90 percent perspiration.

But if this is the logical part of literary creation, there is another, both mysterious and unfathomable, that I do not relate to the vagueness of inspiration, a word often used as a pretext for postponing work while waiting for Godot — something, in olden days, called The Muses.

That mysterious part of creativity is dreaming.

I can plan, the night before, the next morning's work and go to bed peacefully though impatient to get up and renew my writing. But when I sit down the next morning, the plan outlined by my literary logic goes off on a tangent, suffers too many exceptions, and is invaded by the totally unforeseen.

What has happened?

It happens that I have dreamed. And it so happens that the dreams I remember are repetitive, commonplace, and useless. I cannot but think, then, that the creative hand that is guiding my own the next morning is the hand of the dreams that I do not remember, dreams doing their invisible chore: displacing, condensing, re-elaborating, and anticipating, in the dreamwork, the literary work.

Now, each one of us has his or her own way of swatting flies, and mine is to get up at six in the morning, write from seven to twelve, exercise for one hour, go out and buy the newspapers (what they have to say always seems older than my imagination), have lunch with my wife Silvia, read for three hours in the afternoon — from three to six — and then go out to the movies, the theater, the opera, friends.

This is possible — I hastily add — in my literary fortress in London, a well-organized city. In Mexico City things are different. You have so-called political breakfasts — rituals of power brokering, trading information, destroying reputations, advancing others — from eight to ten-thirty. The eating is heavy, as if there were no politics without *pozole*. Lunch is from three to six under the ironic eyes of the Aztec goddess Coatlicue, assuring that digestion will be a difficult task. And then there are the Exterminating Angel dinners from ten at night until two in the morning.

If I manage to write an Op Ed piece under these conditions, I feel well served.

But Mexico — my friends, my family, my marvelous, courteous, tender people, my strangled, asphyxiating city where the air is no longer clear, the territory of my memory and a political life in which reality constantly surpasses fiction — does fill my vessels of communication and renew my creative juices with a fiery diet of tequila and enchiladas.

I can then return to London and be thankful for the bad climate, the awful food, and the cold courtesy of the islanders, without losing my nostalgia for nine hundred varieties of chilis and seven types of *mole*, and treasuring in my ears the two constant sounds of Mexico that are like the daily applause of my country: the hands of our women shaping corn tortillas and the hugs of our men slapping each other's backs.

COMMANDMENT NUMBER TWO:
READ

Read a lot, read it all, voraciously. Fernando Benítez, an old friend, the great chronicler of the Indian cultures of Mexico, had calling cards that simply said: *Fernando Benítez, Reader of Novels.*

My generation in Mexico, and throughout the Latin world (including Italy, France, Portugal, and Spain) was probably the last one to feed its imagination reading the marvelous books that transported us to other worlds, the universe of childhood dreams. They were central to us, but unknown in the Anglo-American world. Emilio Salgari and the tales of Sandokan, the Tiger of Malaysia; Paul Feval and the hunchback Lagardere; the swashbuckling tales of the Pardaillans that permitted us to sport capes and swords instead of overalls and marbles; or the sentimental *Cuore* by the Italian Edmondo d'Amicis that authorized us to cry without shame.

These were the initial books of Latin childhoods, from Rome to Buenos Aires and from Paris and Madrid to Mexico City. But then we added the books we shared with the Anglo-America world, notably Dickens, Stevenson, and Mark Twain, and two giants of the universal imagination, Dumas and Jules Verne. But we were as ignorant of Nancy Drew and the Hardy Boys as gringo kids were of Salgari and the Black Pirate.

Are any of these authors read today, or do children spend all of their time playing Nintendo? I don't know, but I don't believe that is so. My British publisher takes me to the corner of her library in London and from her window shows me a queue, four blocks long, of kids from seven to eleven with ten pounds in their fists, waiting to buy the latest Harry Potter volume. Initial printing: a million and a half books. Expected printing: six million copies.

And a modern version of a Norse epic poem of the seventh century, *Beowulf*, has in the luminous translation by Seamus Heaney become a best seller throughout the English-speaking world.

In Latin America, all through my life, it was a sign of identity and proof of social advancement in the working, student, and middle classes to read Neruda and Lorca, García Márquez and Cortázar, Rulfo and Paz.

The writer is the pioneer of reading, the protector of books, the insistent gadfly: the price of a book must not be an obstacle to the reading of a book in poorer countries or poor classes. Let there be public libraries, open to all. Let young people know that if they lack money to buy books, there are public libraries where they can read books.

This, I am aware, is a lesson well learned in the United States. It has yet to be implemented in Latin America.

Which takes me to my third consideration.

COMMANDMENT NUMBER THREE:
TRADITION AND CREATION

I join them because I profoundly believe that there is no new literary creation without the support of the previous literary tradition, in the same way that there is no tradition that survives without the juices of new creation. There is no T. S. Eliot without John Donne — but from now on, there is no John Donne without T. S. Eliot. Yesterday's writer thus becomes today's author, and the present-day writer is tomorrow's author. And this is so because the reader knows something that the author ignores: the reader knows the future, and the next reader of *Don Quixote* will always be the first reader of *Don Quixote*.

The bridge between creation and tradition lies in my fourth proposition.

COMMANDMENT NUMBER FOUR:
IMAGINATION

Imagination is the madwoman of the house, said the Spanish novelist Pérez Galdós. A madwoman who does not stay in the attic as she does in Victorian fiction but opens wide all the windows, respects the vampires sleeping in the basement, but flies out and raises roofs in Madrid, Mexico, or Manhattan to see what truly goes on in bedchambers and chambers of state.

Imagination flies and its wings are the writer's eyes. The imagination sees, and its eyes are the memory and the prophecy of the writer. For the imagination is the union of our liberated sensations, the sheaf that joins together the disperse, the nature of the symbols that permit us to cross jungles — Dante's *selva selvaggia* — more savage today, perhaps, in cities than in the jungle itself.

To imagine is to transcend, or at least to give some sense to, experience.

To imagine is to transform experience into destiny and to save destiny from mere fatalism.

There is no nature — *natura* — without the bucolic imagination of *Daphnis and Chloe* by Longus, of Montemayor's *Diana* or Spenser's *Shepherd*, all of them pleasant forms that contrast with the terrible, untamable nature of Melville's *Moby Dick* or the desolate urban nature of Eliot's *The Waste Land*.

But the character of literary nature consists, not only of reminding us that the worlds surrounding us can be agreeable or cruel, friendly or unfriendly, but in creating, through the imagination, a second literary reality from which the first, physical, reality can no longer divorce itself.

COMMANDMENT NUMBER FIVE:
LITERARY REALITY

Which means that literary reality is not limited to a servile reflection of objective reality. It adds to objective reality something that was not there before. It enriches and boosts primary reality. Imagine — try to imagine — the world without *Hamlet* or *Don Quixote*. We would not tarry in understanding that the Prince of Denmark and the Knight of the Sorrowful Countenance have as much or more "reality" than many of our neighbors.

So literature creates reality yet cannot divorce itself from the historical environment — physical, chronological, geographical, imaginative — in which it takes place. That is why it is important to distinguish literature from history given the premise that follows: History belongs, strange as it may seem, to the world of logic, that is, the zone of the univocal: the Napoleonic invasion of Russia took place in 1812. Literary creation, on the contrary, belongs to the poetic universe of the plurivocal: What contradictory passions agitated the souls of Natasha Rostova and Andrei Volkinski in Tolstoy's novel?

Literary works — a poem or a novel — shoot out in many directions. They do not demand a singular, unique explanation or, much less, a precise chronology.

Let us read the excellent Russian historians of the nineteenth century, but let us try to imagine that same century without Tolstoy or Dostoyevsky, without Gogol or Turgenev. That is, *War and Peace* does not happen only in 1812. It is reborn on all the battlefields of the war of time; it happens in the reader's mind and there it inscribes itself as a fact of the literary imagination, which, in turn, determines the relationship of the work to time, through the event we call language.

COMMANDMENT NUMBER SIX:
LITERATURE AND TIME

Literature transforms history — what happened on the battlefield of Waterloo or what happened in the bridal chamber of Natasha Rostova and Pierre Bezhukov — into poetry and fiction.

Literature sees history, and history subordinates itself to literature because history is incapable of seeing itself without language.

The Iliad, according to the Italian philosopher Benedetto Croce, is the proof of the original identity between literature and history. It is, he wrote, the work of *un popolo intero poetante*, a whole poetizing people.

That unity has been lost. Modernity is fragmented; it is individualistic. It has not tolerated anonymous collective poetry (or painting or architecture) since Montaigne said, "To be known is not enough; now we must also be renown." The poetic and collective anonymity of Homer did not require this. Victor Hugo does not require it for, according to Jean Cocteau, Victor Hugo was simply a madman who thought he was Victor Hugo.

The epic universe of antiquity is like Gogol's Petersburg, a gigantic animal broken into a thousand pieces. The unity of Homeric language is lost. Hector and Achilles, in *The Iliad*, speak the same language. After *Don Quixote*, one can speak of language only in the plural. Cervantes overcomes lost unity by discovering plurality. Don Quixote speaks an epic language; Sancho Panza, the language of the picaresque — that is, the anti-epic. Ulysses and Penelope can understand each other. Madame Bovary and Anna Karenina cannot understand or be understood by their husbands. They speak different languages.

The breakup of unity thus becomes the unity of ruptures. There is no communication without diversification, and there is no diversification without admitting the existence of The Other — he or she who is not like you or me.

Language thus translates into levels of language, and literature into a reelaboration of hybrid, migrating, *mestizo* languages in which the writer uses his language to throw light on other languages. So proceeds Juan Goytisolo in Spain, contaminating the purity of the Castilian language with a revival of Jewish and Arab roots, or Gunter Grass in Germany, bringing sense and truth back to a language debased by the Third Reich, or the mere multicultural hyphenation of the English language in the United States, as employed by the Afro-American Toni Morrison, the Sino-American Amy Tan, the Mexican-American Sandra Cisneros, the Cuban-American Cristina García, the Puerto Rican-American Rosario Ferré, or the Native-American Louise Erdrich.

God takes his sabbatical before Nietzsche declares him dead, and in his place — God's, not Nietzsche's — appears Don Quixote. That is, the novel appears, no longer as an illustration of well-known truths, but as a search for unknown truths. No longer as the bearer of the antiquity of the past but of the novelty of the past.

I come back to the idea that the next reader of *Don Quixote* shall always be the first reader of *Don Quixote*. The past of literature becomes the future of literature. But also the eternal language of literature.

The language of the original myth that roots us in the lands of our births.

The epic language that pushes us out of the land we know to the worlds we ignore.

The tragic language of the return to our home and the family wounded and divided by passion and by history.

Literature, finally, restores the lost community, the *polis* that demands our political words and actions; the *civitas* that needs our voice as an act of civilization so that we may learn the art of living together, coming closer, loving one another, supporting one another in spite of the cruelty, the intolerance, and the bloodshed that have never abandoned the shadows of a human mind illuminated, in spite of everything, by the light of justice.

Literature gives to the city the unwritten part of the world and becomes a meeting place — that is, a common ground — not only of character and plots, but of civilizations (Thomas Mann), languages (James Joyce), social classes (Balzac), historical eras (Hermann Broch), or *imaginary* eras, as the Cuban writer Lezama Lima called them.

Literary language, in this sense, is a language of languages. It is language regarding itself because it is capable of regarding the languages of others.

COMMANDMENT NUMBER SEVEN: TRUE CRITICISM

Once published, the literary work ceases to belong to the writer to become the property of the reader. It also becomes an object of criticism. And when I say "criticism," I speak of an art neither superior nor inferior to the work under consideration, but rather its equivalent. A critique at the same height as the work criticized. A dialogue between the work and its critique.

For this reason, the best literary critics are the best literary creators. The critical co-respondence, say, between Baudelaire and Poe, Sartre and Faulkner, Georges Bataille and Emily Brontë, transforms the critique into the equivalent of the literary creation. But the great professional critic — as different from an author writing about another author — reaches the same co-respondent relationship: Michel Foucault and Borges, Donald Fanger and Gogol, Bakhtin and Rabelais, Leavis and Lawrence, Barthes and Proust, Van Wyck Brooks and Hawthorne, are but a few examples of this fruitful co-respondence between critic and book.

Thus I distinguish true criticism from mere reviewing — the majority of opinions one reads in the press — or even from undercover criticism — the critic who reads only the cover of the book and then proceeds to authoritatively destroy it.

I recommend that the young writer not occupy or preoccupy him- or herself excessively with newspaper reviews. But let's not be hypocritical about this. We are grateful for praise. We deplore negative opinion, and we admire Susan Sontag because she does not read good or bad reviews. But to subject oneself to either is a mistake. They fade like a whistle. Or, as we say in Mexico, "Le hacen lo que el aire a Juárez." Put in American terms, that would mean that Washington could not be dissuaded from crossing the Delaware.

Let the writers console themselves by remembering that there is no statue, anywhere in the world, honoring a literary critic.

Furthermore, an activity that can be noble and necessary is sometimes diminished by those who practice it while moved by envy or frustration. But the paradox — or, if you prefer, the dilemma — stands. Only in literature is the work of art identical to the instrument of its criticism: language.

Neither the plastic arts, nor music, nor film suffer from this incestuous relationship between creative word and critical word. Not even theater, which is an art of live, but distanced, representation.

Commandment Number Eight: Be Loyal to Yourself

This is my recommendation for the young writer. Do not let yourself be seduced by immediate success or by the illusion of immortality. The majority of seasonal best sellers soon lose themselves in the sands of oblivion, and today's bad seller can be tomorrow's long seller. Stendhal is a good example of the second case. *Anthony Adverse*, super best seller of the year 1933, of the first case. That same year Faulkner published a nonseller that became a long seller: *Light in August*.

Well, eternity, said William Blake, is in love with the works of time. Works of time are *Don Quixote* and *One Hundred Years of Solitude*, and eternity fell in love with them from the very start. But Stendhal's *Charterhouse of Parma* gained only a handful of readers when it first appeared, and that thanks to Balzac's generous praise for a work considered strange and difficult in its time. Destined, originally, for "the happy few," today it enjoys the eternal and renewed glory of generations of readers.

The lesson: Be loyal to yourselves, listen to the deep voice of your vocation, take on the risks of being both classical and experimental, and remember that there are no longer any dogmas for either tradition or renovation.

There is no vanguard because art conceived as the companion to novelty has ceased to be news, because novelty, in its turn, was the companion of progress, and progress has ceased to progress. The twentieth century left us with a stricken, deeply wounded sense of progress. Today we are aware that scientific and technical achievements do not assure the absence of moral and political barbarism.

The artistic response to the political and economic crisis of the modern has been a practically unlimited freedom of style that permits the artist to write in the style he or she prefers. But on one condition: that freedom never forget what it owes to tradition, and that tradition never forget what it owes to creation.

COMMANDMENT NUMBER NINE:
CONSCIOUSNESS OF TRADITION AND CREATION

I come back to the beginning of my Decalogue with this commandment: the consciousness the young writer must have of both tradition and creation. T. S. Eliot, of course, has written the definitive essay on this subject.

Let me distinguish, nevertheless, two slopes. One is the social position of the writer placed between past and future in a present that does not permit escaping the political climate. I do not say this in the manner of the obligatory Sartrean *engagement*. I say it in the name of a citizen's free option.

The writer complies with his social obligation by keeping both imagination and language alive in his writing. Even if the writer has no political opinions, he contributes to the life of the city — the *polis* — thanks to the flight of imagination and the root of language. There are no free societies without writers, and it is not fortuitous that totalitarian regimes immediately try to silence them.

And yet, standing in the public square, alone with his notebooks and his pen (as is my case), or with their PCs (as most today), the writer is giving life, circumstance, flesh, and voice to the big, eternal questions of men and women in our brief passage through earth.

What is the relationship between freedom and fate?

In what measure can we shape our own destiny?

What part of our lives is adaptable to change and which to permanence?

And finally, why do we identify ourselves by the ignorance of what we are — a union of body and soul? We cannot answer. But we go on being exactly what we do not understand.

So, literature is an education of the senses, an indispensable school of intelligence and sensibility through the medium that most distinguishes us from and in nature: the Word.

COMMANDMENT NUMBER TEN

The tenth commandment, therefore, is that I leave in the hands of each and every one of you your imagination, your word, and your freedom.

Margo Glantz

(b. 1930)

(in conversation with Noé Jitrick)

Corporeal Writing

Mercury is Margo Glantz's sign. Not the Mercury of astrology, but rather Mercury, the god of travel; mercury, metal in flux. Glantz is an inveterate traveler of both physical and metaphysical spaces. Her writing, creative and critical, is like quicksilver: gleaming, fascinating, a flashing play of words and ideas that resist familiar categories. Intellectual and editor, professor and successful administrator, she acted as director of publications for the Department of Public Education and as literature director of the INBA, the Instituto Nacional de Bellas Artes. She was, in addition, founder of the journal *Punto de Partida* and served as Mexico's Minister of Cultural Issues in London. She has had a distinguished academic career and has been a visiting professor in many universities in North America and Europe. Perhaps her most prestigious honor was being inducted into the Academia Mexicana de la Lengua in 1995. Glantz is only the fourth woman in a century and a quarter to have gained entrance into that august group, a crown that she wears with circumspection and confidence.

Glantz is a creative critic, illuminating her subjects with the light of her intelligence. Her essays cover a broad spectrum of major literary figures, from Don Juan to Michel Butor, from Octavio Paz to Frida Kahlo. She has published three books on the legendary Sor Juana Inés de la Cruz: *La comparación y la hipérbole* (1999), *Sor Juana Inés de la Cruz, Hagiografía o autobiografía*

(1995), and *Sor Juana Inés de la Cruz, Saberes and Placeres* (1996). One might say that Sor Juana smiled on Margo Glantz in 2003, when she won the Sor Juana Inés de la Cruz prize for the best novel of that year; the elegant work, *El rastro*, that Julio Ortega has described as "the metaphor of the enamored heart," bears as epigraph a line from a famous Sor Juana sonnet, ". . . my heart, dissolved and liquid in your hands."

Heart, hands, tongue, feet, hair: Glantz's fiction and nonfiction have always revealed her fascination with the body. In a brief essay, Jean Franco notes a few of Glantz's obsessions: "In her book of 1983 [*La lengua en la mano*], written in a still-sexually restrained society, she embraces not only eroticism but pornography and sexuality, revising the meaning of the ass (in Bataille), the womb (in Armonia Somers), and the nose (in Djuna Barnes), at the same time pointing out the erotically tongue-tied language of Mexican literature when it refers to the woman's body."

On a simple, not theoretical, level, Glantz analyzes her sense of her own body as owing to "a problem of fragmentation," adding that she writes "about different parts of the body to effect a kind of reintegration. Because although I have no profound wound, I always fancy myself fragmented. And writing is a way of putting the body back together—working on feet, or hands, or sometimes hair." In jest, she explains that she came about her foot fetish because her father was, among other occupations after coming to Mexico, a shoe salesman. The story of her father, of her family, is told in *Geneologías*, her most personally revealing book, an intimate study of exile and assimilation. A first-generation Mexican, a Jew in an overwhelmingly Catholic society, a woman in an overpowering male-oriented culture, Glantz's sense of alienation is not surprising. "Maybe these genealogies will help me understand this feeling. It may date from the day my father brought Susana a Shirley Temple doll from the United States; she was dressed in an orange-and-white silk pajama with an embroidered dragon. Envy drove me from my paternal home."

Whatever has driven Margo Glantz has taken her far.

This conversation between Margo Glantz and Noé Jitrick took place in Mexico City on November 27, 1991, for publication in *Siglo 21*. The two writers discussed various literary topics related to their work, and the transcription reflects the colloquial nature of their dialogue.

———— 🜸 ————

NJ: Let's start our conversation — I'd prefer not to think of it as an interview — by talking about how you decided to become a writer.

MG: I always thought that to be a writer you needed to have good handwriting, but I was always hooked on reading. When I was a little girl, I always got a 5 or a 6 or even a 0 on my penmanship exercises.

NJ: Do you think that there's a relation between those two things? Wouldn't this be a question of graphology, the significance of the stroke?

MG: Yes. In fact, yesterday in New York I went to an exhibit of objects from Freud's house in Vienna. They were things that he'd collected and there was a wonderful text about Moses written in longhand, a hand so perfect that it corroborated my old idea . . . all you need to be a good writer is good penmanship; what's more, good penmanship alone will produce a brilliant writer.

NJ: That old impossibility came back to you.

MG: If I don't have good handwriting, I can't possibly be a good writer. . . .

NJ: But at that long-ago moment you weren't thinking of Freud as a model: he's a model for action after the fact.

MG: You're right. I'm constantly thinking about many retrospective models that haven't worked for me.

NJ: What were your previous models?

MG: English penmanship, the Palmer method; all day long I did exercises with a penholder, a pen, and an inkwell, and those exercises always turned out disastrously for me. There were always smudges. My "graphomania" has to do with the smudge and with graffiti, adolescent graffiti.

NJ: Maybe that weighed so heavily that your texts are never smudged, because if there's one thing that characterizes your texts it's cleanness, in the sense of development, structure, reasoning, the accumulation of images. For me, smudges would be messy, matted, disordered images that led nowhere —

exactly the opposite of your texts. Maybe you turned your initial difficulty into a challenge and resolved the conflict.

MG: Perhaps I have good mental graphology.

NJ: I wouldn't know about that, but [. . .] when you told me about your visit to Freud's house I immediately thought of a text that Mallarmé wrote in longhand, one I saw in Bloomington, in the Indiana University library. When you were a little girl, though, you weren't thinking of either Mallarmé or Freud as a model. What models did you have for thinking about being a writer?

MG: I really didn't have any models, except grade-school teachers who made us copy those Palmer manuals in round letters so we could write like good little English girls, the way you Argentineans still write. We did this every day, and anyone who didn't write well had to write a hundred times, "I'm a dirty little girl, I don't have good penmanship, I can't even copy the letter 'A.'" I just gave a lecture at Princeton about the relation between penmanship and writing by women. Sor Juana complains bitterly in a recently discovered letter to her confessor that not everyone accepts as authentic (I do), about how the simple fact of having more or less decent handwriting was considered *in*decent by her superiors in the convent, and how this made a nun consider it her duty to write sloppily because, according to Sor Juana, her superiors said that it was unseemly for a nun to have good penmanship. The nuns, however, were good accountants, and even though they were not to excel in good penmanship, some of them surely wrote good numbers, in addition to doing handwork like sewing, embroidery, and open work.

[. . .]

NJ: This topic interests me a lot, because it suggests that the stroke, as Derrida would say, has a social distribution, a history [. . .] .

MG: At different times in history, penmanship itself, and the practice of writing, divided the sexes and the social classes, and it also determined rather rigid hierarchies, placing people in particular situations. The writer as a separate gender, the gender of writer, is fascinating. In English museums it's wonderful to see the notebooks filled with the handwriting of English authors. There's a sampler made by the Brontë sisters that any little girl who prides herself on being decent, and who aspires to being a schoolteacher, should be able to match. That's why I'm thinking now about what will happen if I become famous. How will people be able to decipher my handwriting, especially if I'm writing on the computer? That's why I print hard copy and then make notes and scratch things out on the pages, so that the pages will be saved and worth their weight in gold!

NJ: The computer also promises that sort of complexity. People used to study the original at its various stages, and you could tell something about the production of a text by analyzing the different drafts. Now, on the computer, the traces tend to disappear.

MG: I like to make different versions, not so much because I'm thinking about fame and posterity as because I like to see the different steps and what it is that I've been refining.

NJ: Margo, let's go back to the point that led us from writing as penmanship to the moment when you decided to write, when you broke through the barrier of your possible ideals. In fact, let's go back to something even earlier. What kind of ideals have you forged and what do you think made it possible for you to become a writer? When and in what circumstances?

MG: I wouldn't call them ideals; I'd call them permanent obsessions that are always present in relation to my body, or rather, to fragments of my body, my hands, my feet, my hair, my teeth, fragments that are also present in other writers, for example, in Thomas Mann, or in Flaubert. Somehow I fall into a certain kind of textuality that ends up sort of suctioning me in. That's why I don't so much *put things* into writing as I become *submerged in* writing. Right now I'm fascinated with the question of the nuns' corporeality and the way that spiritual exercise ends up becoming body writing, because flagellation, or mortification, as they called it then, follows the method prescribed by San Ignacio de Loyola. It's body writing that is also real writing, done at the confessor's request in what at that time were called notebooks, and then "deciphered" by the friars who transcribed it in journals and transmitted it to other, superior, prelates up the voyeuristic chain. I want to work on that process in both an essay and a novel — for me there's no difference between writing a novel, an essay, a short story, and the texts that I call "fissures." The fissure, by the way, allows me to work with the very Barthean idea that the idea resides in the interstice, in what is never complete, what you find in a rupture, a hollow, a curve, an orifice, as Bataille did, and as Barthes explained in his essay about Bataille. I'm referring to the migrations of the text. That's why I'm working on the kind of constructive writing that hides the writer by building over her a verbal tumulus, a structure of words. It's a literary structure but one that we assume is simultaneously a structure of piety, a pious reading from the pulpit, the confessional, and the procession. I'm coming to unexpected conclusions and I want to work with this same discourse in fictionalized characters. Some nuns, some martyrs from the first centuries of Christianity, were tortured because they did not accept the rules of the pagan religion in Rome. Not only were they beaten, stoned, and burned, not only did they have their breasts amputated, they were *scratched*. I love that image because scratching is a very particular form of writing, where you work with the penholder and the pen and you scratch the paper; besides, it makes a sound. I've just seen *Prospero's Books* by Greenaway; it's based on Shakespeare's *The Tempest* and it's rather flawed, but the idea's magnificent. Prospero is on his island and he's reciting Shakespeare's verses while at the same time he's writing them on parchment in dazzling sepia-colored handwriting, and the sound gives me the shivers, that scratching of his pen on the paper.

NJ: A strumming.

MG: A *scratching*. Because it suggests the wound, and it's related to a particular kind of what you called strumming — the scratching you hear in the basso continuo line in some baroque harpsichord music.

NJ: There's a logic to that, a coherence, because flagellation or mortification implies a mark on the body and this undergoes a series of translations until, as you mentioned, it becomes a text.

MG: Of fissure? Of scratching?

NJ: No, of elevation. What was the word you used?

MG: Construction.

NJ: The unsophisticated reader sees construction only in the moral sense of constructive or edifying, but you're recovering a whole circuit of production here, from that marked corporeality to the constructive, moral sort of message. At the same time, though, your questioning about the nuns would be like a return to an initial moment of writing, I'd say an almost archaic moment, in order to understand, I suppose, your own writing, to understand metaphorically your own body markings as they're expressed in the work you've written since, work in which the genres are, of course, indistinguishable, and in which whether something's an essay, novel, story, or fissure becomes unimportant, now that the overwhelming need is to turn a process begun long ago into writing.

MG: In addition to literary genres becoming fragmented and diffuse, a fundamental element arises in my search for the female body, and that's the fact that marking the feminine body in the tradition of Christian hagiography is a way of removing its individual difference, rendering it indeterminate, sexless.

NJ: Undifferentiated.

MG: Undifferentiated like the body of the archangels. I'm really fascinated by the topic of the archangels because of the absence of difference and the absence of any mark. They're clothed bodies, bodies that have never been touched; they're the ones who do the touching. For example, Gabriel at the Annunciation and Michael destroying the devil turned into dragon. Figures that never undress, about whom, in spite of everything, there's a hint of the indetermination associated with the neutral, the hermaphrodite. It seems to me that there's a certain symbolism in what you just called *undifferentiation.* Curious, isn't it? I'm trying to define feminine writing and I end up using that term so many critics like when they're discussing Sor Juana, that neutrality of the soul within the writer that's expelled by gender but which returns, sexed, in the writing. That's something that in reality I don't accept, but I have to rework the contradiction that I'm outlining here in our conversation. Something even more curious. In the Mexican National Archives there's a place, a section of the catalogue titled *indiferentes,* where they keep undifferentiated papers. I want to work with all of this and from there move from one text to another, and I want to make a text about my own body. In this collection titled "The Whole Body," I want to describe, scratch, a body that's quartered, quartered violently. We'll see if I can do it; it has to be a parodic, ironic text.

NJ: [. . .] At the Ufizzi I saw works by Leonardo and Michelangelo, and I had a very vivid feeling that for Michelangelo divinity was androgynous. [. . .] I've found that Michelangelo said this himself. There's something of the spectacle about the topic, about homosexuality. His biographers point to homosexuality as the origin of his idea about divinity, in the form of projection, since if the painter is homosexual he tends to make the figure or the idea of divinity androgynous. I don't think so — it's a question of something theological. Homosexuality is something contingent.

MG: I'm working with exactly that discourse, with the martyrs, nuns, and mystics. I think that if gender is transgressed when one writes, it's not transgressed in reality; people try to transgress the body and eliminate gender, but I don't think that it's possible. On the contrary, gender gets emphasized, and this leads to the contingency of homosexuality or heterosexuality. I think that it's a strategy of the Church, which is essentially masculine and searches hypocritically for chastity in asexuation, although even if it's quite obvious that there were some homosexuals, and that homosexuality is not why things — the androgynizing of the soul and the bodies — happened the way they did. No, there was a very special preoccupation with woman in that society that was apparently so patriarchal. People have tried to explain this in various ways, but I don't think they get to the bottom of it; there's something more, because woman's power is great. Lucy Irigaray has studied this, and Josefina Ludmer mentions it with respect to Sor Juana, but I think there are things that no one's worked on, at least in this area where I'm digging, scratching. There are very subtle ways of escaping that control, ways for women to avoid becoming undifferentiated, asexed.

NJ: There's a saying, a commonplace, synonymous with Byzantinism, that when you ask about the sex of the angels, angels would be "not different" by definition, which implies that it would be absurd, useless, to try to determine their sex, the kind of thing you'd expect from someone who has all the time in the world — to waste. But when you talk, you're referring to gender, to masculine or feminine.

MG: I'm also referring to genre, though, literary genre; I'm talking about writing itself, which originates in the body, which is sexed.

NJ: Perhaps, but let's make that separation to start; let's leave aside distinctions between the literary genres, the dramatic and the lyrical, and talk about gender as it's understood now. Many people have found it upsetting to think of writing as a sexed product, not so much the fact of being able to recognize their sexuation in writing but being able to mark it, define it, being able to say why some particular writing is feminine or not.

MG: I think that this is always something cultural, because if good handwriting is feminine in one age but in another age beautiful feminine hand-writing is indecent, we're sent back to a single nucleus: writing done by a woman's hand is worthless, a special, ritual, social hierarchization that belongs to a particular age. But what interests me is this: the problem of the sex of the angels, rather, the sexual indifferentiation of the archangels leads me to another problem, but I'll come back to that later.

NJ: First, though, let's see if it would be possible to describe writing that's feminine or masculine, without leaving out what you've noted so well about the fact that the topic arises from handwriting itself. Handwriting is the basis; then there are texts in which there is no handwriting, in which images and structure are the important things, texts in which there's fiction, poetry, in other words, everything that we know texts to be. How would one go about characterizing writing as feminine in order to differentiate it from masculine writing?

MG: Tamara Kamenszain studies this issue very thoroughly with respect to Lezama Lima, for example, in what she calls the basting threads in the text. And people have often remarked that Artaud or Bataille or Barthes, among others, are writers who write with a feminine sensitivity, but up to that point it's more a question of writing that approaches feminine sensitivity because it involves a disarticulation of discourse totally opposed to the masculine tendency toward the epic.

NJ: There's a sort of superego that, in the case of feminine writing, would be more destabilized, more dialectic.

MG: I'd say that there is also a superego in feminine writing, but it's obviously different from the masculine superego. Man's superego is usually directed outward, and that of woman toward the house, the intimate, although in a certain way toward the simple, the apparent, as well. This would need to be explored more thoroughly.

NJ: But your idea of the fissure would be a concept that would make it possible to synthesize many things. It's already a feminine idea in itself, because the word "fissure," which in man can be objectified in an image that's almost geological, is not the same for woman.

MG: That's where I was headed. At the conference in Taxco on the dis-courses of art, I met an Italian critic, Mario Perniola, who has an essay about Lucas Cranach and the nude in Renaissance painting. Just yesterday in New York by chance I saw a small painting by Cranach, a nude feminine figure, a woman somewhere between Eve and a courtesan. She's wearing several garnet necklaces and a veil that reveals her but still separates her from the viewer; the woman is standing beside a tree — there are several of Cranach's paintings in which this placement is repeated: a naked woman wearing necklaces, at the foot of a tree; the woman is touching or pointing to the tree, in which there's a kind of split. The split and the veil have a symbolic meaning that can be deciphered in liturgical terms, because Christ's body is somehow related to the feminine through his open wounds. The need we were talking about earlier with respect to the nuns' having to strip woman of her sexuality, to make her an undifferentiated body, also produces a sort of "hermaphroditization" of Christ's body, and has been studied a lot in the context of the plastic arts by Perniola, for example, or Catherine Bunyon. I'm finding this very compelling because it has to do with the idea of the split in a woman's body, which is simultaneously a fissure and a gash — that's what Octavio Paz calls it in *The Labyrinth of Solitude* — and writing starts from that. One writer who saw this very clearly was Barbey de'Aurevilly, a Decadent who's not much read, but who has some extraordinary texts, for example, *The Crimson Curtain*, *Le Chevalier de Touches* [The Knight of Touches], *Bewitched*, books in which woman is seen in relation to the writing of her blood, which circulates in the text — a femininity hidden within but, simultaneously, always present, externally verifiable from without.

NJ: I'd like to turn again to your own work, though, if we could.

MG: I think that in an increasingly conscious way my writing is approaching what I've always wanted to do. Of course the execution is increasingly difficult, but each time that I complete a text, it becomes valuable. I'd like to be able to finish an entire series of textualities that are only thought out, formulated, but not yet written. I already have some bits and pieces that I've written in the past, and a rough outline, in the sense of an anecdote, but I still can't write it. What I was saying about constructive writing would fit in this context. A great book would be the book of shoes, the tragic story of a woman, of a great love that ends paradoxically with one totally grotesque element and another that is lyrical and tragic — but that's only for the person who suffers it, never for the reader.

NJ: The tragic thing would be the secret circulation of the text, and the writing would be parodic.

MG: The story would be tragic from the point of view of biography, but ultimately the transformation into writing must, of necessity, be parodic, never tragic. To a certain extent, this points to grotesque tragedy, without my ever wanting in any way to approach the Bakhtinian carnivalesque, which has been worked over ad nauseam by superficial critics. The way that Bakhtin has been trivialized is intolerable, and anyone at all feels perfectly within his rights to appropriate him or to turn his ideas into a monstrosity and make them banal. I think that Bakhtin could be applied to the Mexican baroque, but one would have to study this; for example, the idea of the clown.

NJ: The disguise can be carnivalesque, but not all disguises are.

MG: Venice, Casanova . . .

NJ: We could say that the author hides, but in a series of successive disguises. In a historical novel, it's very difficult to find the disguise the author has adopted in the text. [. . .]

MG: I'd put it like this: You want to unveil something extraordinary. However, if you could do it, the thing would no longer be extraordinary. Like the transparent, tenuous veil that must cover a naked Venus, who at the same time is wearing ruby necklaces and a deep red velvet hat. And there's a tree, too, with a mysterious split and a whole host of symbols that in spite of their transparency disqualify transparency. There really is no transparency; there's a need to denude, but nudity requires fissures and veils. I'd like to write another novel, and if I could write a book of memoirs of the body, I'd be ready to die — a book about the coronation of Popea, not according to Roman history but exactly the way that Monteverdi saw Popea and Nero at the end of his life, through a wonderful amorality, handled from the voice of the contralto; again, the problem of indifferentiation.

NJ: Of course, the voice that approaches the masculine.

MG: Yes, the castrato, who played Nero in Monteverdi's opera. It's a contralto who plays that role now, and again we find ourselves in that game of the undifferentiated, but through Monteverdi, the creator of a modern opera with a very particular life, and with Seneca's stoic character in the middle. Marvelous, and that extraordinary Sforza court. Imagine: Seneca in the middle of an amoral libretto, and with undifferentiated voices, marvelous, enveloped in that harmonic contralto. If it only turns out the way I'm thinking about it.

NJ: It would be an excellent illustration of that idea.

MG: The problem is that art in general tries to visualize. For example, in plastic language, a secret you know is fundamental, though without knowing what that secret is. But then I ask myself, why go on when Kafka already did it masterfully in a brief text, the different versions of Prometheus. In short, you try to get hold of it through your obsessions, your fictions, your essays, your . . . but it's never really where it should be, because in the fissure you find nothing, only whatever surrounds it and . . . well . . . we'll leave it at that. It's like orgasm: you never know where it's going to lead; it's like the definition of God is for the mystics . . . orgasm as the craving for God. I'd give up everything, body and everything that provides me with a sense of reality, in order to write about that reality, because that's the only thing in life that interests me. Sounds sappy, doesn't it? Well, as my mother would say, that's how it is.

Translated by Carol Maier

Elena Poniatowska

(b. 1932)

A Question Mark Engraved on My Eyelids

"I write to belong," she begins.

Elena Poniatowska's life, the immediate history of her family, reads as if it were the script for a dramatic novel or a film. In the swings that often occur from generation to generation, we might speculate that the fictional quality of Poniatowska's reality caused her to gravitate toward her style of writing: writing based on fact, everyday but often uncommon real events and real people. Poniatowska refers to her trademark manner of narrating as "testimonial literature." It is a mode reminiscent of the New Journalism of Norman Mailer, Truman Capote, and Tom Wolfe, although it developed quite independent of and earlier than that genre of North American literature. For fifteen years, newspaper journalism was Poniatowska's major expression (she has more than once asserted that she was assigned interviews because it was a task not sufficiently important for male reporters). Journalism was a perfect training ground, in addition to a passion in itself. "You get hooked. There's an old saying, 'When that viper bites, administer last rites.' It fills your head. Some internal convulsion makes you sweat ink."

One brilliantly edited and written book reporting the events of a particularly egregious event in the 1968 student uprisings in Mexico City, *La noche de Tlatelolco* (in English, unlike the straightforward original, *Massacre in Mexico*) has passed fifty editions, and an absorbing testimonial novel, *Hasta no verte Jesús mío* (Here's to You, Jesusa), is approaching that number. In 1988 Poniatowska published *Nada, nadie: Las voces del temblor* (Nothing, No One: Voices from the Quake), another example of her testimonial literature, using the personal witness of hundreds of survivors of the 1985 earthquake that devastated a large part of central Mexico City to document the horrors of the event and its aftermath.

Poniatowska's inherent feminism is seen in her strong female protagonists, for example, the talented Italian photographer, Tina Modotti, whose story appears under the title *Tinísima*; the title character of *Gaby Brimmer*; and most vividly, perhaps, Jesusa Palancares, the central figure of *Here's to You, Jesusa*. She has written a score of presentations for books of photography—*Women of Juchitán* is a classic—and has contributed a myriad of prologues and essays that demonstrate her empathy with other female artists.

What literary genre does not appear in Poniatowska's *curriculum*? It would be difficult to find one. Novelist, poet, short-story writer (one of her most recent publications is a group of eight short stories published under the title *Tlapalería*, a very Mexican word for a hardware store), essayist, interviewer, reporter, and biographer (her sensitive biography of Octavio Paz was published in 1998) it is clear that Poniatowska is a kind of literary phenomenon.

When a well-known Mexican journalist, Braulio Peralta, asked Octavio Paz, "What is the role of Elena in Mexican literature?" he replied, "Well, if you are in a park where there are a lot of people—children playing, laborers on their way to work, sweethearts kissing, policemen patrolling, vendors of this and that; there are lovers, wet nurses, mothers and old women knitting, there are vagrants reading newspapers or maybe a few reading a book, and there are birds. . . . Well, that is Elena, she is a bird in Mexican literature," the bird who observes it all and then sings her song.

I write in order to belong. My family on my mother's side (my great-grand-mother, grandmother, and mother) were always traveling. They had lost their land during the Mexican Revolution, but they still had enough money to live in Biarritz, then in Paris, and later in "Fairlight," England. (I would much rather have called it "Wuthering Heights" but "Fairlight" it was, sweet and *comme il faut*.) They would travel from Karlsbad to Lausanne, from Marienbad to Vichy, to "take the waters." They would get off at a station, stay for a week, then get back on the train. They would see the switchman grow smaller and smaller, his lantern turn into a firefly. My grandmother's house was filled with portraits of Goethe and Wagner, and with books in German; she loved Germany. Mamy-Grand, who was a very young widow, was called "the Madonna of Sleeping Cars," because she took so many, so very many trains. She always dressed in black, her white milky throat and décolletage illuminating the blackness of her veils and *crêpes de Chine*. Later, in Mexico, I would pause on Venustiano Carranza Street, before the window of a shop that sold outfits for a woman's ideal state: widowhood. I never tried on a wedding gown, but I did try on widow's clothes. Widows used to go around the way the poet Jaime Sabines would like them to: "There is one way, my love, that you could make me completely happy: die." Now widows are not even merry.

The traveling companions of Elena Iturbe de Amor were three little girls in ruffles, petticoats, ribbons, and hats, their little faces lost amidst billows of embroidered cloth: Biche, Lydia, and Paula — my mother. The nanny who stands behind them in the photographs was also covered in starch and crepes. Mamy-Grand would carry her samovar with her (because my great-grandmother, Elena Idaroff, was Russian), as well as her silk sheets to put on the hotel beds. It's not that we were gypsies, although we do have some of that in our blood, it's just that we seemed not to belong. Biche still wears strings of pearls dangling about her stomach and her chains remind me of railroad tracks.

From sweet France, the land of the handkerchief-size gardens (*lieu commun*) and of tender vegetables that fit in the palm of your hand (peas are also pearls), I arrived in an enormous plain surrounded by mountains and live volcanoes, traversed by buzzards that would circle around and then suddenly swoop down to feed off the carcass of some skinny little donkey. A land of corn, hard, yellow corn, like large teeth, that women grind on a stone into tortillas. Not just the *metate* and *molcajete* — the grinding stone and mortar — but many things in Mexico were stonelike: the expressions on people's faces and the windowless houses that looked like small pyramids all curved into themselves. As a young girl, it seemed my eyes would burst trying to reach as far as the horizon. The stern, dark-green magueys would come marching toward us, goose-stepping like German soldiers. It was a fearful and splendid country; from up high one could see a little train crossing the valley with its colored-pencil smoke, a lone toy amidst the vastness of the landscape. I knew that I wanted to be part of it, to step into the painting, stand on the mountaintop, be the girl on the edge of the precipice and have a twentieth-century José María Velasco paint me there.

One way of belonging was to listen, to see faces, to take them into oneself, to observe laps, hands. I liked to spend time in the warm kitchen, fragrant with spices; the toasted chiles would make us cough; the boiling milk was always on the verge of spilling over. I would follow Felicitas to the rooftop (rooftops are the realm of servants), where she would wash her long, long black hair with "chichicastle," a small, green, foaming herb. For years I would go with her to the market. I would sit on park benches to wait for her while she kissed her boyfriend. They were such long kisses! I was enormously curious about the servants' lives, and about the villages they left behind to come to Mexico City. One of them, Epifania, had epileptic seizures that terrified me, especially because she didn't want anyone to know about them. Later, when I read Dostoyevski, I was in familiar territory, so I loved him all the more.

I absorbed Mexico through the maids. A system still persists in Latin America which consists of privileged people having at their beck and call the poorest of the poor. In some space within their bodies, perhaps in their unbraided hair, maids are extraordinarily free because they expect nothing; they leave the minute they want to. And alongside their everyday life of garlic and onions, they have a mysterious and magical life, which grows in an inaccessible, arrogant terrain that can be as haughty as the realm of their masters.

In my country today, one doesn't have to be very wealthy in order to have the services of someone who doubles as washing machine, dryer, garbage disposal, salad mixer, vacuum cleaner, and bed-maker, who responds with a human voice, and who even says thank you when she gets her meager salary. When I was a child, the servants' lives and miracles fascinated me, because they didn't keep the distances that European maîtres d'hôtel and chefs do. On the contrary, I discovered Mexico through them, and not even Bernal Díaz del Castillo had better guides. Surrounded by Malinches (Malintzín, the Indian woman who gave herself to the conqueror Hernán Cortés, thus betraying her race), I was able to enter an unknown world, that of poverty and its palliatives: teas and potions that could ward off even the pain of the soul; herbs for stale air; eucalyptus to clear the lungs; the bitter *tolache*, a tea which they say drove the empress Charlotte mad, when she tried in vain to have Maximilian's death sentence commuted. The same Maximilian that my mother loves, because not only did he say "Soldiers, aim at my heart," but he also saw the deep blue sky of Querétaro, found it beautiful, and said that it was a good thing to die on such a day.

Without realizing it the maids provided me with a version of Benito Juárez; they were all like Benito Juárez. Like him they vindicated themselves: "Dirty foreigners." Like him they defended Mexico, as stubborn as mules. Like him they had no roof of their own and had eaten only poor people's food, and for me, a girl raised on French mashed potatoes, discovering them meant entering into "the other." I have always wanted to lose myself in others, to belong to other people, to be the same as them. It is always the others who are right, who hold the key to the enigma. Since then, my capacity for entering the lives of other people has been unlimited, to the point that I could no longer hold myself back, define my limits, much less define myself. To this day, if I ask so many questions, it is because I don't have a single answer. I believe I will die like this, still searching, with a question mark engraved on my eyelids.

Perhaps this sense of not belonging made me a writer. As for the questions, I have interviewed more than a thousand people, from Henry Moore to Luis Buñuel, from Barry Goldwater to André Malraux, from Gabriel García Márquez to William Golding. *What, when, how, where*: the answers are always surprising, because in Latin America reality surpasses fiction. Journalism traps one. It fills one's head; an internal trepidation makes one sweat ink. Cyril Connolly was right when he said that art needs clean hands.

To write in Latin America has a different meaning than it has in the United States or in Europe. I suppose the same happens in Africa. Latin America invades, possesses, interferes, gets into the smallest crack. Latin America is always out there, behind the window, watching spying, ready to jump. The street enters through the door, people find their way in, look at you while you are sleeping, eating, or making love. The path is public. In great American cities, everyone has something to do, people go some-where, walk quickly, never turn their heads to look at their neighbor. In Latin America, in Mexico, no one has anywhere to go. Thousands and thousands of people with nothing for themselves. Nothing. Not a single oppor-tunity. Their empty hands hang near their bodies, in front of their mouths, or on top of their knees, their waiting hands without any use. All this human energy is there, wasted. They look, they wait, they look, they doze, they wait again. Nobody loves them, nobody misses them, they are not needed anywhere. They are nobody. They do not exist. So much to do in the world, and there is no place for them, so much lost energy. There is no one to tell them, let's get up, let's get going, let's save, let's build. Outside my window, the multitude is always present, ready to burst in. Life is very resistant. People — the same cannon folder that nourishes great universal misfortunes, "the wretched of the earth," as Frantz Fanon called them. Suddenly, during an earthquake, one of them saves a life. We have no idea who he is, what his name is, no way to thank him, he doesn't expect to be thanked, we will never see him again, he saved our lives, or murdered us — maybe it doesn't matter, maybe it's the same — he is there, latent, frightfully present.

In the United States, I suppose that people are in the back of a writer's head, in the back of their minds. In Europe also, they sit there waiting to be picked up as characters in a story, in a novel. In Mexico, people are settled in the front of our minds; they never go away, they are always waiting, expect-ing. Isn't it then an absurdity to write? María Luisa Erreguerena, a young Mexican writer who wrote a delightful and witty story, "The Day God Got in Bed with Me," doesn't write anymore. She became a doctor.

For instance: there was a football game in Mexico City. People tried to get in, they were crushed to death in the tunnels. A father came out, the corpse of his son in his arms. Before, between El Salvador and Honduras, there was a football war. Because of a game, the army of El Salvador invaded Honduras, the air force bombed four cities, and, in retaliation, Honduras tried to penetrate El Salvador; thousands of men were killed.

The people of Honduras and El Salvador are completely alike, same height, same complexion, same poverty, same color; all of them are accustomed to misfortune. During the student movement in 1968 (the same as in Berkeley, Paris, Nancy, Tokyo, Prague) more than four hundred Mexicans were killed. In Latin America, stadiums are built for games, but they are also used as concentration camps, as jails, for public trials, and in 1985, after a devastating earthquake, they were transformed into morgues where people could go and claim the bodies of their dead relatives. This isn't to say that we Mexicans have the monopoly on all the sufferings in the world and that I think myself as the universal widow of all afflictions, faithful to my youth's vocation. But it is true that it is different to be a writer in Latin America and in Africa, more than in other countries.

It is difficult to follow up a multitude but in my huge country no one waits to become part of a novel. People jump like rabbits into vowels and consonants and they stick their ears out. And their teeth. The first time I saw Jesusa, I knew she was going to eat up all my words. In 1963, I had what I believe was the fundamental meeting of my life, with Jesusa Palencares, the protagonist of my book *Hasta no verte Jesús mío*. She was less than five feet tall and the years had made her smaller, rounded her shoulders. She had lost her beautiful hair, for which she once had been called "Reina Xochitl!" (Queen Flower) by the soldiers of the Revolution. There were brown stains on her hands; she said they were due to her liver, but I rather thought they were from the passing of time. With time, men and women are gradually covered by mountain ranges and depressions, hills and deserts. Jesusa increasingly resembled the earth; she was a mound that walks, a clay pitcher dried in the sun. When I met her she was fierce. "You say you want to talk with me? With me? Look, I work and if I don't work I don't eat. I haven't got time to chat, least of all with strangers."

It was true. She didn't need anyone, she was enough for herself, she completed herself, alone, she was her other half. One of her main topics was always "the rent" and she moved out many times. On each occasion she ended up farther away because the city tosses out its poor, getting rid of

them, pushing them out, throwing them away as far as possible. Her last
home had no drainage, no water, no light.

I think about her with reverence. I love her. I talk to her inside my heart.
Inside my head. My breasts love her; because of her I also love being a
woman, I who, at age fifteen, wanted to be a man. Jesusa gave me a hard time
at first. I won her over little by little. She began to tell me the story of her
nomadic life in the Revolution. She was part of a multitude. I asked her sev-
enty-seven thousand questions. She answered patiently, then she became
irritated. She just couldn't understand how someone with schooling could be
so ignorant, so slow to catch on. She was right. She didn't like the final version of the novel; she asked me not to bother her with that fucking thing
again and, above all, not to put her name in it. Jesusa led the way. Neither of
us insisted, neither of us forced the other to say anything. We never referred
directly to the act of love. I asked for no explanations. She knew humanity
well and had no faith in me: "The interest is yours, not mine. You'll come to
see me as long as you are able to get something out of me. When you don't
need me anymore I'll never see the likes of you again." One night she
repeated: "Some day you will come and you won't find me; you'll find only
the wind. This day will come and there will be no one to give you any information, and you will think that everything has been a lie. It's true, it's a lie
that we are here, the stories they tell on the radio are lies, the neighbors tell
lies, and it's a lie that you are going to miss me. If I am of no use anymore,
what the hell are you going to miss? And in the factory also. Who will miss
me if I'm not even going to say goodbye?"

Jesusa greatly influenced my life, because she has never asked anything of
anyone. She has never been a subordinate although her life was so hard. As
she demanded a great deal of herself, she taught me to follow her down the
road. We are here in order to serve. We are sent here to earth by God, and if
we are bad, we will return time and time again in different forms to atone for
our guilt. Jesusa used to say that she must have been a very bad, drunken man
who had abused women in an earlier life, in order to suffer as much as she did
in her last reincarnation.

I would like to return to earth because I love life. I would like to gaze,
even from afar, on the grandchildren of my grandchildren and on everyone's
grandchildren, to see the trees, especially the "pirules" (American pepper

trees) and the "sabinos" (Mexican cypresses), the city square of the Zócalo "where the greatest storm fits," the sea on the coast of Oaxaca, the turtles that Francisco Toledo paints, his grasshoppers, the rabbit that laughs, and the fox that pokes fun at us all. I would like to go back holding Jesusa's hand, both of us young and strong, able to walk the whole road. I would like to see her smoking a "Farito" slowly, very slowly, holding it between her thumb and her index finger; I would like to offer her an aged tequila, a glass of water left out in the night air, a green lemon.

I feel that I didn't do her justice with *Hasta no verte Jesús mío*; I obeyed her, faithful to the point of exacerbation, hanging on each of her gestures like a person in love. The images that I have of her are painful, they wound me. Because of her I underwent a process of self-examination. I had the feeling that I was stealing her words and that, in exchange for the treasure that she was unknowingly placing in my hands, I would not even be able to offer a portrait of her essence. No one on earth has given me what Jesusa offered me. No one of my social class has ever said to me what I have heard from Jesusa, no one with her features, no one with her wisdom — the wisdom of corn and wind. While she picks up sticks and paper and old rags and bricks to build her house, we debate on the psychiatrist's couch. To be a troop follower, a *soldadera*, is to walk with the soldiers, to prepare food, to participate in the campaign. Jesusa, for example, gallops next to her husband, Pedro Aguilar, and while he shoots she loads his Mauser. When he dies, she is the one who shoots. She gives us fulminating images, unforgettable ones of what it means to fight. In Mexico, life isn't worth anything and when he falls off his horse, she doesn't notice it at first, so brutally simple is death. "I was still handing him his Mauser and since he didn't take it, I looked over but Pedro was not on his horse anymore."

In Mexico, we are accustomed to calling poor Mexicans "Indians." Indians, the Mazahuas, the Nahuas, the Mayas, the Otomíes who sell chewing gum in the streets; Indians for being indigenous and carrying out the humblest tasks. In this sense Jesusa is Indian: she comes from Oaxaca, she's dark skinned, and for years she worked as a maid; her parents were peasants and the land holds no secrets for her, although she never went back to her province. In contrast to Mexican women peasants she does not remain silent; she speaks out. In contrast with other Mexican women peasants, she had no children of her own, but she picked up stray children and dogs in the streets, fed them and taught them how to work, hit them to teach them "education" like she had been taught. And loved them.

Jesusa led me to social problems and to my writing books like *Massacre in Mexico*, about the student movement in 1968; *Strong Is the Silence*, the story of land seizures in the states of Morelos and Guerrero, and peasant struggles for land, political prisoners and hunger strikes; *Nothing, No one*, against the Mexican government, its incompetence and its corruption, and for the people's courage during the earthquake in 1985; and *It All Began on Sunday*, with drawings by Alberto Beltrán, a book on the holidays of the poor, their Sundays sitting in the streets watching the cars go by and, if they are lucky enough, riding on merry-go-rounds. Carefully I asked them questions, visited them in their crowded neighborhoods, watched their kites cross the sky in February, treated them like kites, because that's how testimonial literature is. It fills one with anxiety, with insecurity. One handles very fragile material, people's hearts; their names, which are their honor; their work; and their time. And one tries to turn it into memorable material. I never imagined that Jesusa would become a well-known literary character, nor did I foresee that *La noche de Tlatelolco* (*Massacre in Mexico*) would be read by the young. Books take on a life of their own and they find their own destiny. That is the sorcery of literature.

I have always walked. I think as I stroll along: How much of me there is in these faces that don't know me and that I don't know, how much of me in the subway, in the steps that pile up, one on top of the other, until they finally come out into the great, white spout of light, how much of me in the last, weary steps coming out, how much of me in the rain that forms puddles on the pavement, how much of me in the smell of wet wool, how much of me in the rusted steel sheets, how much of me in the Colonia del Valle-Coyoacán buses that rush along until they crash and form part of the cosmos, in the graffiti on the walls, in the pavement, in the earth trod on a thousand times. How much of me in those worn-out benches, their paint flaking, how much in the hardware stores, in the little corner stores, how much in all those testosterone shots on those dusty pharmacy shelves, in those syringes that used to be boiled and that spread hepatitis, how much of me in the signs that used to hang all along San Juan de Letrán: "All types of venereal diseases treated," how much in the newspaper stands, in the Fountain of the Little Frogs, in the shoe-shine boxes, in the rickety trees — just like little sticks climbing up to the sky — in the man who sold electric shocks, in the old people's wrinkles, in the young people's legs.

The women in my family share a peculiarity, the absence that others call distraction. We are never really there. In her middle age, a doctor friend used to give Biche such tedious explanations that she claimed, "I don't listen to him. I think about something else." My mother has always thought about something else. For her, coming back to reality must be like stepping into a coffee grinder. I believe that my mother could only accept her suffering over her one son's death through her capacity for evasion and, especially, through her faith. My brother is better off in Heaven; who knows how things would have turned out for Jan if he had continued on earth. Wrapped in scarves, ethereal, with her long neck and her elusive gaze, my mother, the most beautiful of all women, is the one who most inspires my love, because I have never been able to reach her. Now, when she wants to give herself to me, I return her to her niche. No, no, don't do it. The curtain is lifted by the wind and I cover my eyes.

I have always responded to challenges, followed apocalyptical personalities, apostles, Rasputins, Joans of Arc who hear voices that come from Heaven, illuminated guides of humanity, holders of truth, priests. During my childhood I was marked by competition amid the worn desks, the purple ink of the government school in the south of France. I dutifully accepted the repressive atmosphere, even though inside myself I sensed something subversive that I would have to let out: a joy at daybreak, as if a sun were going to burst from my mouth. But when? How? One of the reasons why I married my husband was because he was an astronomer. He would explain to me what it all meant, he would tell me why we are here and where we are going, our reason for being. We would become, our three children and myself, part of his universe. We would belong. Once again, the problem of belonging.

I live to the rhythm of my country and I cannot remain on the sidelines. I want to be here. I want to be part of it. I want to be a witness. I want to walk arm in arm with it. I want to hear it more and more, to cradle it, to carry it like a medal on my chest. Activism is a constant element in my life, even though afterward I anguish over not having written "my own things." Testimonial literature provides evidence of events that people would like to hide, denounces and therefore is political and part of a country in which everything remains to be done and documented.

Some Latin American writers inscribe our literature within a collective project. In this respect Carlos Monsiváis and I are just two more Mexicans out of the 84 million that now exist, and a smidgen of the 103 million that there will be by the year 2000. Our reality is therefore infinitesimal. It is barely a dot, the head of a pin within the sea of heads that covers our territory, like in that photograph of men in hats that Tina Modotti took during the 1920s, a sea of hats, a sea of heads, each head a world. Mexico between each person's ears. Mexico is a country of young people. Since 1980, one and a half million young people have entered the labor market, and our country has not created the twenty million jobs that are needed for the other unemployed and underemployed Mexicans. Even today, we know that there are fifteen million hungry people.

In spite of these voices, every morning in Mexico I get up to life without knowing what it is. Also to literature. Nor can I decipher the enigma of my country, nor that of my children, let alone everyone else's children. I have always had questions, and to this day, I don't have a single answer. I simply don't have any. I look for them in other people. In their words, in their acts, in the expressions on their faces. Sometimes at a party, some eyes will encounter mine, just a blink. I really loved the sidelong gaze, green and yellow like a parrot, that my father used to turn on me. My father was my son, just as today my son Mane is my father. Of Polish origin, he used to cry. Poles cry. Mexicans almost never cry. Machos never do. He loved my mother like the first Poniatowski loved Catherine the Great, who made him King of Poland in order to get rid of him. He wrote her passionate letters. "I don't want to be king, I want to be in your bed." Perhaps he wasn't a very good lover, but he was a gentle king. My father never knew how to ask anything of anyone. In Mexico his heroism was his secret. He never formed part of any chorus. One had to grasp him intuitively. It was on the piano that he expressed himself best, but at age seventy he stopped believing even in musical notes. When he died I knew that he was inside me, that I would become him, as all my dead are in me.

What will Felipe and Paula do? What will they be? What can one do with this bundle of uncertainties that knocks around inside one's head?

I have always been drawn to characters like Jesusa Palancares. María Sabina, the one who performed the ceremony of the sacred mushrooms (LSD in Oaxaca), Juan Perez Jolote (the Chamula peasant from Chiapas), Demetrio Vallejo (the railroad leader), all popular heroes, even if they are not recognized. I admire them because of their wisdom and the way they impart it, with great patience, great prudence, with respect for the ignorance of the person who asks the questions. That the poorest Mexicans don't deserve their ruling class is a truth that leaps out at once.

For Stephen Spender, the Spanish Civil War in 1936 was a war of classes, on an international scale; the capitalistic class, backed by international imperialism, against the democratic will of 80 percent of the Spanish people. In 1990, the reality of Latin America is not very different from Spender's Spain. In Latin America, wars are class wars, on one side the oligarchy linked to the military class and the great capital, and, on the other, the poor people, the ones who have nothing to lose. Fear of communism in 1936 is still flagrant in 1990. And more absurd, more mediocre.

Writers in Latin America live in a reality that is extraordinarily demanding. Surprisingly, our answer to these demands protects and develops our individuality. I feel I am not alone in trying to give their voice to those who don't have it.

In 1979, for instance, Marta Traba published *Homérica latina*. Marta Traba was a very sophisticated and well-known art critic, a sort of "enfant terrible" at the Museum of Modern Art in Colombia. She was brilliant, original, and feared. She died in a plane crash in Aeropuerto Barajas in 1980. To me, *Homérica latina* was a surprise, and a still greater surprise was *Conversación al sur (Mothers and Shadows)*, about the political situation and the mothers of the Plaza de Mayo in Argentina. Marta Traba had suddenly changed. Multitudes took over. Multitudes invaded her. No art museum could close the doors. *Homérica latina* is a novel in which the characters are the losers of our continent, those who pick up the garbage and live from it, the inhabitants of the slums, the masses who trample on each other to see the pope, those who travel on the crowded buses, those who cover their heads with straw hats, those who — like Jesusa — have nothing to lose except their lives.

They take their dead children to be blessed and photographed so as to transform them into "holy little angels." They tumble down the platforms of military parades and, suddenly, without trying, cause all the policies of good neighbors to fail. This anonymous mass, obscure and unpredictable, is slowly populating every corner of Latin America; the people of the bedbugs, the fleas, and the cockroaches, the miserable people that at this moment are gobbling down the planet. This formidable mass extends and crosses frontiers; they work as porters and mechanics, ice cream vendors (why do our countries have so much ice cream and so many sodas?), and cleaners of anything and everything, errand boys and shoe-shiners. José Agustín, a young Mexican writer, once declared that in the United States they believed: "I'm a shoe-shine boy made good." It would have been better for him to have said "a shoe-shine boy made bad." We have all been made bad, we are all needy, all unwanted guests around the feast, invited at the last minute. In recognizing this lies our creativity.

Translated from the Spanish by Cynthia Steele,
to whom the author dedicates this essay

José Emilio Pacheco

(b. 1939)

Poems

In Mexican letters, José Emilio Pacheco is classified as belonging to the post–Octavio Paz generation. He does, chronologically, and it is a generation he has made his own. Pacheco may be the most reclusive of men, perhaps the least self-promoting writer on at least two continents, but it is clear that he has been sought out for honors. Poet, essayist, novelist, short-story writer, journalist, translator—the list of his prizes documents his talents in those many fields: Aguascalientes National Prize for Poetry, 1969; National Prize for Journalism, 1980; Malcolm Lowry Prize for Literary Essay, 1991; National Prize for Literature and Linguistics, 1991; José Asunción Silva International Prize for Poetry, 1996; José Donoso Ibero-American Prize for Letters, 2001; Octavio Paz Prize for Poetry and Essay, 2003; Ramón López Velarde Interamerican Prize for Poetry, 2003; Pablo Neruda Iberoamerican Prize for Poetry, 2004; the Alfonso Reyes International Prize "for a literary career," 2004; the Premio Ibero-americana de Pablo Neruda, 2004; and the Premio de Poesía García Lorca, 2005.

Pacheco is articulate and intelligent, but his resistance to the idea of discussing himself and his work is a phobia of long standing, one he expressed in 1982 in a poem published in *Trabajos del mar* (Labors of the Sea) and titled "Una defensa del anonimato" (Defense of Anonymity), which was written "to avoid being interviewed."

A pact with this writer who offers us the opportunity to make "his" poem "ours" may be a difficult engagement, for themes of despair and world disintegration thread through all his works. It is an opportunity, however, we would be foolish to turn away from.

Taciturn though he be, José Emilio Pacheco has in his writing more to say *about* writing, as we see in selections from *Tarde o temprano: poemas 1958–2000.*

[*How shall I explain . . .*]

How shall I explain to you that I have never
    granted an interview,
that my ambition is to be read, not "famous,"
    that it is the text that matters, not its author,
that I am leery of the literary circus. . . .
To begin this non-response, I shall tell you
I have nothing to add to what is in my poems,
    nor interest in commenting on them; I am not
concerned with (should I have one) "my place in history"
I write, no more no less. I write. I offer half the poem.
    Poetry is more than black signs on a white page.
What I call poetry is the site of that encounter
    with another person's life. The reader, man or woman,
will make, or not make, the poem I have merely sketched. . . .
A strange world, ours; every day
there is more and more interest in poets
    and less and less in poetry.
The poet is no longer the voice of his tribe,
    the one who speaks for those who do not speak.
He has become just another entertainer:
    his sprees, his fornications, his clinical history,
his affiliations or quarrels with the other clowns in the circus,
    the trapeze artist, or the elephant trainer,

have assured a wide audience
    of people who no longer need to read poems. . . .
I keep thinking
that poetry is something different:
    a form of love that exists only in silence,
a secret pact between two people,
    almost always two strangers. . . .
In fact, the poems you have read belong to you:
    To you, their author, who invents them as you read.

Matter Consumed

Syllables, return to my lips, words
that name and reconstruct the forgotten.
Touch anew, words, the servitude
in which your fire burns itself out.

Then, song, return once more to the place
where time blazes as it flows.
There is no mountain or wall to stay its passing,
the everlasting, not the instant, flees.

Now I name you, fire, and in your flames
I recognize myself; I saw in your white heat
the destroyed and the remote. It was

a short-lived tree in a jungle of ash,
word that recovers in sound
the consumed matter of the forgotten.

Acceleration of History

I write a few words
    and within minutes
they are saying something else,
    communicating
a different intent,

submitting docilely
 to Carbon 14:
Cryptograms
 of a far distant people
finding their way to writing
 in darkness.

Poetry: a critique

Here before me repetitious rain and its wrathful brambles.
Salt, the sea distilled . . .
He erases the preceding, then writes
This convex sea, its migratory
and deeply-rooted customs . . .
already the inspiration of a thousand poems.

(Mangy bitch, pustulous poetry,
laughable assortment of neuroses,
the price some pay
for not knowing how to live.
Sweet, eternal, luminous poetry.)

Maybe this is not its time.
Our era
has left us talking to empty air.

Job 18:2

How long will it be ere ye make an end of words?
God — or his scribe —
asks
in the book of Job.

Yet we keep polishing, wearing away
an already dry language: attempts
to make water burst from the desert.

Dissertation on Consonance

Sometimes, because of the sonority of Spanish, it seems
that poems still proceed in accord with meter.
Though starting from, and treasuring, and plundering
meter, the best that has been written in the last fifty years
has little to do with Poetry as it was defined by
academicians and theoreticians of another time.
So, then, there must be proposed to the assembly
a new definition that will expand limits (if they still exist)
some dictum less permeated with the invincible challenge of the
      classics.
A name, some term (suggestions are accepted)
that will preclude the shock and wrath of those who
. . . so very reasonably . . . read a poem and say
"This isn't poetry."

Personal Experience

Those forms that I see by the seashore,
the ones that immediately engender
metaphorical associations,
are they instruments of inspiration
or fallacious literary quotations?

Legitimate Defense

If learned critics publicly deride
My verse, well, let them.
Not for them I wrought.
One day a man shall live to share my thought,
For time is endless and the world is wide.
BHAVABHUTI, TRANSLATED BY JOHN BROUGH

I

The Sainte-Beuve of our village died.
His heirs auctioned off the Great Critic's books.

Out of curiosity I went to the sale.
I found all my books there, with the pages uncut.
His ridicule of my poetry has become classic.
Because of his opinion, I have always been an outsider.
Rest in peace, *Indefatigable Reader!*
    [1939]

2

They followed the latest trends.
They were, all their lives, in the vanguard.
They attacked everything that was old.
I remembered their names
when I read tonight in the newspaper
that the Academy had recently honored
its exalted Life Members.
    [1951]

3

He could not be called my antagonist
or my rival or my enemy:
simply a contemporary.
We seldom speak.
From a distance each of us sees in the other
the speed with which our entire generation
is aging.
Just as the style
we thought eternal
is now history,
an unpopular past,
a restraint and an obstacle
to young writers
who — if they notice us at all —
gift us with
a snicker or sarcastic remark.
    [1937]

4
Said Samuel (perhaps not realizing
that he was quoting):
"I write to be admired
in the year 2000. And my words
will live forever."

Thirst for immortality.
I looked outside:
in the garden a vile fly was struggling
to extract nectar and pollen from a flower.
An impossible task
at this point
to try to become a bee.
   [1949]

5
Did you ever think about your enemy,
about the one you don't know
but who loathes
everything you write?

Have you thought about that young man in the provinces
who would give his life for your death?
   [1942]

6
(Taste of the Time)
Every poem is a living entity:
it grows old.
   [1952]

7
(To Poets Yet to Come)
You must be implacable.
(So don't be forgiving of my errors.)
Our weaknesses will give you strength
and you will succeed where we failed.

But once we are expunged
(if we are remembered at all)
I hope you will realize
that perfection
is forever beyond the grasp of human aspiration.
   [1952]

8
(Ars Poetica I)
We have a single thing to describe:
this world.
   [1948]

9
(Ars Poetica II)
Write whatever you want.
Say whatever comes to mind.
No matter, you are damned before you begin.
   [1949]

10
(Poet's Monologue I)
I would like to be a radically bad poet,
happy with everything I write,
and live far away
from your self-critical, admonishing
finger.
   [1949]

11
(Poet's Monologue II)
They sentenced to death
all the elegiac poets,
among whom
(too lazy to defend myself)
I am included.
   [1950]

12

(Poet's Monologue III)
Whom do you mean to flatter with those
trite verbal pirouettes,
those dolorous little sighs and word play,
and implied ironies?

Would you like for someone to pat you on the back
for how beautifully your little bells
jingle? — pitiful
paraphernalia of a party
you weren't invited to.

It's better if you hide in dark corners.
Persons like you get no praise,
they're flayed or stoned.
No one's going to applaud
your artful little games.

It would be best, buffoon,
to find your corner
and stay there in modest silence.

Lives of the Poets

In poetry there is no happy ending.
Poets end up
living their madness.
They are drawn and quartered like cattle
(it happened to Darío).
Or they are stoned, or end their lives
by throwing themselves into the sea, or with crystals
of cyanide in their mouths.
Or dead of alcoholism, drug addiction, poverty.
Or, worst of all, as official poets,
bitter occupants of sarcophagi
called *Complete Works*.

Observations

1. Balance
That year I wrote ten poems:
ten different forms of failure.

2. Manifesto
We are all poets of transition:
poetry never stands still.

3. Polaroids
Within a very brief time these poems
will sound more ridiculous than they do today.
There will be no film in the shops,
so my words will fade away,
like out of focus old Polaroids.

4. Poet
Plow in the ocean.
Writing on water.

5. A Love Letter to Amado Nervo
Bad taste is eloquence worn thin.
Don't worry
if we smile at your doleful verses
and today feel we are superior.

Sooner or later
we'll be keeping you company.

6. The Author Declares His Anonymity
My poems do not capture a following.
My books clutter basements.
There is no defense against the *Reader's Digest.*

7. Against Readings
If I read my poems in public
I suck the meaning from poetry:
attempting, for an instant at least,
to have my words be its voice.

8. Conference
I flattered my listeners. I refreshed
their supply of clichés
of ideas appropriate to our times.
I made them laugh once or twice
and quit as soon as boredom set in.
In return, they applauded.
Where
can I hide to cleanse away my shame?

9. Ars Poetica
Not your hand:
ink blindly scribbles
these few words.

10. Scrawl
To write
is, in a certain way,
to live.
And yet, everything,
in its infinite pain,
leads us to intuit
that life will never be written.

Written in Red Ink

Poetry is the shadow of memory, but
it will become substantial, the fabric of the forgotten.
It is not a stela erected in deep jungle

to last amid its decay,
it is grass that shivers for an instant
in the meadow
and then is debris, dust,
less than nothing in the wind of eternity.

Page

Thanks, a thousand thanks, everything is fine.
I appreciate what you are doing, and I thank you.
I like my laptop and my laser printer.
But I am as I am, and not for me are
poems on a screen or in many voices
or with electronic animation.
I will stick (though I be the last) with paper.
The page is not, as it is said now, a *crutch*:
it is the house and flesh of the poem.
It is there the intimate encounter happens
that makes your own body from other words
and makes you one with what the letters say.

Poetry

Against the dark night
a glowing screen
and a blank page.

Against Harold Bloom

Despite what Dr. Harold Bloom writes about influences
I do not suffer from that anxiety.
I do not want to kill López Velarde or Gorostiza or Paz or
    Sabines.
Just the opposite,
I couldn't write, and I wouldn't know how to behave,

in the unthinkable circumstance that there was no
Zozobra, Muerte sin fin, Piedra de sol, Recuento de poemas.

Farewell

I failed. It was my fault. I recognize that.
But in some way I am asking forgiveness or indulgence:
It happens because I am attempting the impossible.

Translated by Margaret Sayers Peden

Angeles Mastretta

(b. 1949)

Dreaming a Novel

It would be difficult to surpass the self-portrait Angeles Mastretta published on the jacket of her runaway best seller, *Tear This Heart Out*.

"Angeles Mastretta was born in Puebla, Mexico, in October, 1949. She studied journalism in the Political and Social Science Faculty of the Autonomous University of Mexico, and did her doctorate in solidarity with lost causes. She is also a professional worrier.

"For the past twelve years she has devoted herself to journalism and literature in the foolish belief that what happens in Mexico is her business. She is obsessed with her children, pines for her father, and now and again fights with her husband, although he is an admirable specimen of the genre.

"She is indecisive, unpunctual, and feels the cold. She sleeps badly and it shows. In the mornings she is absentminded, and in the afternoons she is prone to bouts of melancholy, which are cured by a siesta. She sometimes confuses hunger with existential anguish.

"She is incapable of giving orders and saying no, but finds asking favors easy. She has several bosom friends, and her mother thinks she wastes too much time talking to them on the phone. Like all mothers, she is right, of course. But how else can you love your friends in Mexico City?

"She is inquisitive and so talkative that when there is no one around to listen, she tells stories, writes down her fantasies and memories, and invents characters that get under her skin and absorb other people on lazy afternoons.

"This book wanted to be a political novel but it turned into a love story. The author says she will never be good at anything else."

In the intervening years, Mastretta has continued to write love stories, principal among them the book *Lovesick*, which won Latin America's most prestigious prize in 1999, the Romulo Gallegos. Her children survived their childhood and are following their studies in universities. And she pursues her journalistic interests, writing for magazines such as *Fem* and *Nexo*. If those names suggest a feminist leaning, it is not inappropriate, because she is considered a leading figure among the group of women writers who espouse this cause that emerged in the seventies and eighties. She has colorfully defined her position among them. "In Mexico there are two congregations: daughters of Mary and daughters of whores. I do not sit down to dinner with either group."

Angeles Mastretta has chosen the third option. In her writing—novels, short stories, journals, and newspaper columns, all of them set in her home city of Puebla—she writes her own convictions, with professional discipline. "Did I know I was going to be a writer?" she asks. "No, it wasn't that when I was five years old the Holy Spirit came to me and told me, 'You're going to be a writer.'" But writer she is. And she recently told Fabiola Santiago that she yearns to be like her fictional creations. "Those characters are courageous and disorderly in a world that is constructed for them to be obedient in, timid and quiet. They're women who don't transform reality, but they do transform *their* reality. They decide their own destinies." Mastretta's was to write. Somewhere a *new* novel is being dreamed.

The first time she came to my mind, Emilia Sauri was sitting in her backyard feeding some very white, rather restless, hens. Her skirt was hiked up, exposing long, strong legs — just as they would be later. She had almond-shaped eyes, wide hands, and she smelled of incense and herbs. An early morning moon hovered above her head, and a star was growing between her legs as her feverish imagination invoked a man with whom she did not sleep.

Emilia Sauri would be a woman enslaved by two passions. Domestic yet daring, soft but belligerent. She would have a house filled with children and relatives, a much-desired husband — hard-working and generous as rain — a lover whose story I still had not figured out and did not wish to know, not until the morning when he would burst into the middle of the book — brash and disorderly, with slightly slumping shoulders, his head full of extraordinary visions — and sweep us both, Emilia and me, off our feet.

Fortunately for her, and for me, Emilia Sauri never owned hens. The next time I saw her she was straining to determine whether it was true, or just a dream, that she loved two men at once, with equal ardor, with the same burning desire for each, with nary a concern beyond schedules and dawns. How can a woman love two men and resign herself to wake up with only one of them? Emilia Sauri would ponder this and many other problems that came her way in the life that I was dreaming up for her, starting on the afternoon when her parents, after many attempts, managed to conceive her.

Diego Sauri, her father, was to be a man of the sea, ever burdened by not being within earshot of its roar, since he would live under the shadow of two volcanoes and in the bosom of a stable and comforting woman whose waist would remain small through years of upheaval and multiple loves. Josefa Veytia, her mother, appeared one morning in a café in Veracruz with her tireless sister Milagros.

But all that came much later, long after that Easter vacation when I first saw Emilia Sauri surrounded by hens and was overwhelmed by the fervent desire to write her story. How would it be if, instead of those hens, her father had left her a pharmacy filled with tiny bottles and porcelain jars? I guess my delight in the past thrives around rhubarb syrup and *tolú* pills in a way that it does not surrounded by hens and carrier pigeons. Or was it that when I sought a passion befitting Diego Sauri, he still lived on an island of hushed greenness where a healer was more necessary than a poultry man? How did Emilia come to be born at the end of a century like ours, a century that like all others was consumed by abuse, by hope, by injustice? How would she grow into her prime in the face of war? I cannot really say. So many things happen in a book, so many events, so many worries can fit inside three hundred pages that, when asked about a book I just finished, I panic at the possibility of being able to tell in ten words or less everything that it took me years to recount. Years when I went with uncharacteristic punctuality to the room where I invented tales in order to exorcise its silence. That, more than anything I do, has given me life. I never learned to knit, never had enough talent to play the piano, never fathomed engineering. I would not know how to run a business, or take orders from a group, or a boss; I have zero ideas for saving the earth, and all I know about medicine I have looked up in handbooks as the need arose. I was never able to memorize two lines of a legal text, could never keep the books for a store, and am utterly incapable of selling an umbrella, even in a rainstorm.

This is not to complain about my many deficiencies, since writing is an endeavor that makes up for most. Through my writing these last few years, I have heard a woman's angelic voice — so unlike mine — have fallen deeply in love with ten men, have recovered the father I lost early one morning, have spent time with him and shared his fondness for opera, politics, and good wine, as if he were that pharmacist and I his adoring daughter Emilia. I have been stable like Josefa and outrageous like Milagros Veytia. I have had a rich uncle leave me a grand colonial mansion, and have played by the fountain in my great-grandfather's garden. What is more, I have met him, and from him learned how to heal wounds, diagnose illnesses, even coax babies out of the blue wombs where their mothers carry them. Writing *Lovesick* — the book I finished barely six months ago and that I already miss like a world forever lost — I climbed aboard revolutionary trains, became doctor, healer, fortune-teller, village girl, general, priest, bookshop owner, guerrilla fighter, the lover of a man who needed me and of another who did not know what he wanted. Now that the novel is out of my hands, and has been read by the three readers I fear the most, and the three that are ever forgiving; now that it has been sold to a publisher, and translators' carefully worded inquiries have begun arriving, I am overcome by nostalgia for that beatific world I inhabited while writing, though I was sleeping fitfully, constantly bemoaning my fate, and burdening others with my woes, feeling trapped in a strange and harsh reality that might, or might not, let me go.

What is it like to write a book? What purpose does it serve? Books are solitary objects complete only when someone opens them, existing solely when there is a person willing to get lost in them. We writers are never sure that there will be that someone to give meaning to our labors. But write we do, at times in dread, others with glee, as if skirting the edge of an abyss. Will anyone care? Will someone weep for the deaths that we have mourned? Will there be someone to fear desire, yield to it, and conjure it along with us? Why bother to depict old traditions? Will anyone be moved by the aroma of steaming broth floating down the staircase that an adventurer like Daniel Cuenca is ascending? Who might value the courage of Antonio Zavalza's old-fashioned silence? Is it worth it to pour over ten books about herbs and potions just to find the two words that make half a page believable? Less precise than physicists, more engaged in magic than doctors, we writers work in order to dream about others, to improve our own destiny, to live all those lives that would be denied us if we were to be only ourselves.

I started to work on Emilia Sauri's novel almost a year after seeing her and first yearning to do it. It was January 1993. I decided Emilia Sauri would be born one hundred years earlier, partly because I wished to explore life at that time, those years of great risks, of dreams that now seem remote. I could not imagine a period more different from ours. I did not become aware until much later of how much I did not know about things I had thought as familiar to Mexicans as their own name. What was going on in our country in the years before the Civil War? What exactly was the *Porfiriato*, aside from the thirty years when a man named Porfirio Díaz ruled the land? What did people do, what professions did they choose — those who were able to — and who did not even bother to try? Where did the children of the middle class go to school, what kind of soap did they use, who were their doctors, what medications did they take, what did they do for fun, how did they travel?

Only a whiff of all I learned made it into the novel. Nothing more was needed. Apparently, I did not need to be acquainted with every hero, movement, manifesto, and demonstration that shook the nation between 1893 and 1917. Still, I would not have dared believe my own novel without that background knowledge. Even if, in revising, only a handful of that swarm of details remained. What I did get, while working my way to the present, were myriad reasons for reflection, numberless anecdotes about a past that seems to be playing itself out once more.

I fulfilled my duty of inventing a new world each morning. I wrote in order to feel that I was improving the present by invoking the past, to ascertain that life had been difficult and beautiful many times before, to remember that there is little one can do, although many spend their lives trying, even knowing it is all in vain.

Not every morning was the same, although an observer might have thought so. I sat in the same spot, bent over the same machine, was irritated by the same noises, listened to the same Ave Marias. Each day was either a torture or a feast, and I could never tell in advance. Now, however, I recall that still-recent period with the same nostalgia reserved for long-ago days of wine and roses. In that sense, the creative experience does resemble giving birth. Were it not for the witnesses of my constant wailing — who are there to remind me — I would not remember a single one of the many awful moments, and would readily swear that I was never happier than in the times, the home, the country, of the Sauris.

I find it difficult to talk about my obsession with words, with the way they sound and combine with others, with how many adjectives are enough and which is the perfect one. Those things are what I consider the most secret part of my private life. Having things look natural requires a dangerous sort of artifice. But the total absence of artifice would prove even more dangerous. I am addicted to sounds, constantly in search of words: plump words, warm and comforting. I begin to write thinking that I will not have to revise, though it never fails that I always go back over the text hundreds, thousands of times. I play with it. Originally, I wanted to write a novel about the desires and ambivalence of a woman, and somehow this woman and her desires ended up inside another, less accessible, more complicated story. I imagined Emilia Sauri first as a thirty-seven-year-old woman who does not know what to do about the strange turns of her heart; then, as an old woman who shares her memories with an inquisitive granddaughter. Politics played no part, there were no wars in this story.

In the novel I just finished, however, Emilia Sauri never shares her thirties with us. We do meet her parents, along with their friends, relatives, fantasies, political ambitions, and educational issues. We get to know Emilia the child and the young adult, not the mature woman. We witness the war that played havoc with her life. We do not know if she ever owned hens or how she raised her children. Neither are there any conversations with a granddaughter. Those details were left out despite their being so clear in my head. That is why the book's structure became a problem. I do not recall, because my current quest for tranquility will not allow it, the anguish that I experienced for months on end when, convinced that the novel was getting bogged down with unnecessary details and thoroughly avoidable scenes, I decided to attempt a different structure. There were nights when I woke up certain that after so much editing I had managed to erase the whole thing. Others when I simply could not sleep, wondering if it would be better to devote myself to teaching meditation and dawdling. And there were worse. Some when I was sure that I would not make it even as a beginner yoga student. If on one of those days a family of mice had invaded my house, as it happened this week, I would have gone mad. Fortunately, by chance, the rains proved patient. They waited, not until I finished the book — books are never finished — but until I let go of it.

Many things, terrible incomprehensible things, happened in the country while my head was taken up with a reality that no one cared about but me, that depended on no one but me. Now that for six weeks I have been looking life in the eye without any filters, I shudder at the thought that our future might resemble the Sauris' troubled time. We choose strange ways to deal with the world around us. Now I suspect that choosing the past, looking at it through Emilia Sauri's eyes, walking it in her shoes, has been my way of dreaming that things will work out, that these times are not any worse than those of long ago, that our children will be allowed to pursue their passions, build a future, face their own abysses. Just as our grandparents did, just as we are doing.

Translated by Cristina de la Torre

Alberto Ruy Sánchez
(b. 1951)

The Lesson of the Jaguar

Alberto Ruy Sánchez is a man with two tightly interwoven careers: writing and publishing. The resplendently colored thread that weaves them together is sensuality. The sensual in all its manifestations.

In *Artes de Mexico*, Ruy Sánchez directs what he calls "an encyclopedia of Mexican culture," a collection of art books in magazine format currently consisting of over seventy titles. The aim of this large-format, breathtakingly beautiful publication is to "delve into hidden aspects of the country through its visual manifestations; to be ever curious and inquisitive, incessantly exploring, discovering, and marveling at the new enigmas of a multiform, dynamic, highly creative, and always surprising culture." Each issue covers a single aspect of Mexico's rich store of arts and crafts, from pre-Hispanic times to the avant-garde of contemporary Mexico.

There is a second, and parallel, venture overseen by Ruy Sánchez: a series of books featuring individual artists, visual and literary, studies of various regions and crafts, and a number of informational publications, such as the catalog of the San Carlos Museum, and the Spanish-language *Guide to the Collections* of the J. Paul Getty Museum.

In *Artes de Mexico* one finds the most sumptuous and, at the same time, most educational portrait of Mexico available today.

That is Alberto Ruy Sánchez the publisher, the man whose graceful presentation of sensual surfaces, erotic images, and mythic lands becomes more personal, more intimate in his writings. His invented Mogador, for example, city of desire, serves as the setting for a trio of books: *Los nombres del aire*, *En los labios del agua*, and *Los jardines secretos de Mogador*, a trio of poetic explorations of the universe of his sonambulistic universe.

He has said that he writes "hoping that everything will, sooner or later— or never—lead to an idea of writing as an artisan's tool. An implement wielded with meticulous and passionate concern for forms, something into which one pours everything one is and has." He writes "like someone who holds out a hand to show others a stone he has found in the river, something that pleases and astounds him for its strangeness."

A dozen novels, autobiographical sketches, poems, stories, a bestiary, essays, portraits of other artists, all these genres come to life at that juncture where music, painting, dance . . . life . . . intersect, exploding in bursts of energy and beauty, like the leap of the leopard with which Ruy Sánchez identifies.

I write very slowly, my lips tingling with the taste of words, like someone who eats very deliberately, taking all the time in the world. But I also write as if something were gnawing inside me, filling me with a tension that can escape only in words, in sentences written as if I were singing. On pages scored like musical compositions. I also work, however, the way some Mexican artisans work, patiently seeking the best form for their creation, wanting to take pride in what they have done. Prouder yet if they feel that their piece is imbued with a portion of their souls. I write slowly, but creating a time within time. A radiant, strangely suspended, moment. I write giving each phrase space and time. As if I were preparing a fire that will at some moment ignite. To what can I compare this sensation of something that is expanding inside me, something that flows only as gradually I fill a surface with those smudges we call words? I write feeling that I must let the animal inside me emerge.

This morning I was standing before a jaguar in the Chiapas zoo. It was pacing with strangely solemn, and yet at the same time nimble, steps, from one side to the other of the fenced hill that confines it. It was not like the other animals; one could sense the terrible tension that animated that jaguar. Every step, every movement was menacing. It gave the impression of being possessed, obsessively driven by thoughts and dreams ready to burst through its skin. Suddenly, from the twenty meters that separated us, it focused on me, then raced straight toward me, nearly flying. It gave a prodigious leap. Without emitting a sound, and much before I could blink with fright, it crashed against the wire mesh fence that separated us. It showed me its long claws and its fangs. Then, very casually, it continued its now placid stroll, in the opposite direction. It had taken my breath away for an instant that seemed infinite. My heart was pounding. A shiver ran down my back. In an invisible, but not fantasy, world where more things happen than are seen, my pumping heart was already its prey. I moved to its perception of time. It had hunted and caught me.

I was aware, in addition, that long before its surprise attack, the jaguar had created an area around it invisible to the eye but sensed on my skin, an atmosphere in which its tension dominated as if beneath a well-defined, enclosed cupola. As if beneath a large glass dome. And that aura was larger than the space of its fenced enclosure. I had stepped inside it and perceived the uncommon tension of its body. They say that the ambit created by the jaguar's presence can be felt in the jungle anytime it is nearby. It is not a sensation that arises only from its being caged.

When I write I am filled with something too large to be contained inside me. It is as if something were about to explode. Like one of those captive beasts whose movements reveal the volatility of their dreams and the tension of their desires. A writer is sometimes an animal that creates a palpable space around him, a space that cannot be seen but that is perceptible to initiates: those readers who allow themselves to be trapped in the kingdom of the unseen. Those who permit poetry to capture their hearts and make it race to the rhythm of words sung, measured, and recounted, the rhythm of the marvels conveyed ritually in a poem, like the lope, and the voracious leap, of a jaguar. I write like a jaguar imprisoned, or in rut, or ready to spring. I have learned why in Maya bas-reliefs and stelae the hide of the Jaguar symbolizes invisible forces. And, in addition to the powerful and the warriors, the only figures allotted that special mottled pattern are those who write. In the world of the Maya, he who writes is part of the secret universe and the invisible strength of the jaguar. A condition we contemporary writers cannot achieve at will.

And like the thousand shadows on the jaguar's body, I feel that I write and rewrite for a thousand logical and illogical reasons. Always seeking that vivid harmonic composition we admire in the contrast of dark and light zones on jaguar's hide. My skin, the hide of the animal that writes, is similarly patterned. Among my spots, I must admit that I write obsessively, without discipline but without pausing. Obsession helps me fill in what is lacking and inscribe my creation nearer the reign of pleasure than of duty.

I write the way a persistent artisan concentrates on his material. A ceramist who sees born of his hands forms that seem to have been waiting for decades. Forms that, though physically far away and touched by other hands, will lead me to touch those of friends — or enemies — I do not yet know. I also write like those ceramists who cover walls with amazing geometric tiles in the form of mandalas, with individual pieces that form a puzzle that is at once projected time and invention, plan and rigorous improvisation. Like gold- and silversmiths, I forge tools to the measure of my hands. Like weavers, in threads of capricious and meaningful colors, I recount my dreams and my myths, as well as those of the persons who travel with me through this life. And I write like the potter who entrusts to his kiln the soft object of clay that emerged from his fingers, hoping that fire, in the last, uncontrollable process, will improve it, or at least not destroy it.

I write in order to know, to explore dimensions of reality that only literature may penetrate. I write also to remember. But just as important, I write to forget. I write to stretch my body and my senses. To confirm, day after day, the world's sensuality. I write for pleasure. I write out of desire. I write out of rage. I write to point out the counterfeiting of icons, the abuse of public power. I write to be despised and to be loved; even more, to be desired. I write to propose new ambits in this world. I write to provoke the ritual apparition of Poetry. I write to dance. Dancing is the body's other magical writing. I write to speak with the dead. Especially, with my dead, alive in their literature, in their art, in their works. I write to listen to the living. I write to exercise the enormous pleasure of understanding. I write to draw. I write to erase. I write to smile with lips other than my own. I write to exercise the vitality of the tongue and the sex. I write to seduce my beloved, again and always again, to win her paradise. I write to travel. And my footsteps write with my eyes, and what is outside leaves a trail of capricious letters inside me. Letters of astonishment. I write to capture what flows from me. All that lies ahead, in union with which I will be better. I travel in a thousand ways when I write. And I also write to not move at all. I write to travel inward. I write about myself and my beloved and about the corners of this world that wait to be explored. I write to show myself naked. I write to hide and disguise myself. I write to invent a carnival. I write singing. I write even when I am not writing. And at that moment, too, I search or, without searching, experience the ritual apparition of that sudden existence, that exception that we may or may not call Poetry.

Translated by Margaret Sayers Peden

Carmen Boullosa

(b. 1954)

Daughter of the Park

Carmen Boullosa is a poet, novelist, playwright, and educator. She is also a good example of the cosmopolitanism of the contemporary writer. Born in Mexico City, where she took her degrees, she received a grant to study for several years in Germany, where she was later granted an award by the Berlin Academy of Arts. She is the recipient of a Guggenheim fellowship and is currently a professor at the City University of New York. Although she has probably written more prose than poetry—she is author of more than a dozen novels, a half-dozen plays, and nearly a dozen books of poetry—it is tempting to say that Boullosa is a poet who also writes novels and dramas. The intellectual component of this multifaceted writer can be seen in her work as editor of the *Diccionario del Español de México*. Which, one wonders, nurtured which? Writer or editor?

Boullosa's intimate relationship with poetry is revealed in a recent interview with Rubén Gallo. "I also like to read poetry while writing a novel. I read the poems quickly, drinking them up, gulping them down, as if to get drunk. Poetry recharges my batteries. When I am rushing to finish a novel, I read poets like Lope de Vega, Jorge Guillén, Quevedo, Sor Juana, almost without reading them. They nourish my ear."

Despite her international renown, Boullosa told Gallo, she believes that women writers are still discriminated against in Mexico, and that "the Mexican literary world, afflicted by an ever-shrinking pool of readers, has closed itself off to women writers and to the modern notion of men and women with rights and equal intellectual capacity." Women like Poniatowska, Glantz, Castellanos, *and* Boullosa have had to be strong.

Boullosa often assumes the voice of a male character in her writing, like the protagonist of *They're Cows, We're Pigs*, a stirring novel of seventeenth-century piracy, and of Moctezuma, come back to life in the Mexico City of 1989, in *Llantos, novelas imposibles*. At the same time, much of her writing has the sound of autobiography, such as the character of Delmira, the little girl who is the protagonist of one of her most recent novels, *Leaving Tabasco*, though the basic facts of Boullosa's childhood do not support that reading. No writer, however, can escape the influence of his or her own experiences just as, ultimately, each reader reads his or her own novel or poem.

Introduction (to Salto de mantaraya; a fragment)

I am here, outside, outside, outside,
expelled by the assault of this love
that did not know how, or wish, to harbor me,
that left me without veins, without lungs,
without skin or lips, or words, of course.
I write, leaving myself
here, on the paper. Hearts
blood is ink. Mine
is nearly black, like the sea,
turned dark by banishment and corrosion.
With these writings I shall inhabit myself again.

———❦———

By chance, which can be so generous at times, I was staying in a hotel across from the main park in Bad Homburg, on the outskirts of Frankfurt, in

October 1996. I was there to receive the Liberaturpreis that had been awarded to the German version of *La Milagrosa*, translated with an angel's touch by Susanne Lange.

Not by chance, but because it's almost routine for me, I had spent the night in the throes of insomnia and had run out of things to read. It was a quiet, chilly morning. I still had an hour to kill before my hosts would come to take me I don't recall where. Suspecting that my insomnia would return and catch me off guard, locked away in my cell across from the empty park in a town I was sure had no nightlife, I decided to run over to Bad Homburg's only commercial street to buy a book that would free me from those four walls and make me immune to my insomnia. I had no idea how big the bookstore would be, since the town is tiny but rich in some ways. I decided that surely I'd find something in English and even got into my head that some "novelty" was going to fall into my purse.

To get to the bookstore, I had to cross the park, the one that Novalis, Hölderlin, and other romantics loved. I took long, hurried strides, enjoying, as never before, the park's singular beauty. It's more beautiful than any park I've ever seen.

That morning fall had ignited the park, its long life, its romantic and seemingly disheveled beauty, flooding my heart and body with emotion. Deeply moved, I thought, "Here's my last wish: to visit Bad Homburg Park." This thought was entirely out of sync. Why think about my "last wish" when I'm moving so freely, feeling so healthy, happy, even "larger than life"? It transported me to a memory, to my grandmother, to her voice first of all. I was five or six, in the kitchen, afternoon was falling, my grandmother was roasting banana leaves for tamales on the comal baking dish. She was saying that Epitacio, one of her brothers — like her, from the state of Tabasco — realizing he was dying in Mexico City, had pleaded with his children to "Please! Get me a persimmon!"

Back then, persimmons didn't reach the city. Today you can get them in the markets in Mexico City, of course, but in those days it was impossible. From time to time, a family member brought my grandmother a couple from Tabasco. She would stash them away like a treasure on top of the refrigerator until they were good and ripe. Then she'd cut one open and eat its translucent flesh as if doing so were a miracle. My grandmother ended her story. "And his heartless children let him die without bringing him a single damned persimmon from Tabasco."

I couldn't see my grandmother's face, just her hands as she put the fresh banana leaves on the comal to cook, taking them off half withered but very flexible. A few steps away was the *masa*, ready for the tamales, piled in a mountain-shaped mound on the table. The smell of the banana leaves and the smell of the *masa* were two scents you couldn't mix up. When the banana leaves are roasted, they give off an extremely delicate perfume that is lost when the fire touches their fibers. My sense of smell was aroused. The scent of moisture rising off the leaf as it heats on the comal calls up feelings I can't explain, as if those feelings belonged to someone else, someone very different from me. The *masa's* scent, in contrast, brought me back down to earth. It contained roasted pig fat, "drippings," and maize for the baked *nixtamal*. Next to that was the stew prepared the day before to fill the tamales, colorful but with no aroma on account of its temperature.

Alert and torn between so many scents, I asked myself, "What will my last wish be?"

But I had no answer. The question left me naked before the aroma of roasting leaves, *masa* just mixed, and the light, the light that was dimming. Like Epitacio, I was going to die, too.

I held on to the feeling, my mouth clamped shut, packed tight as the tamales would soon be. Alone that night, after my Uncle Gustavo turned out the light in my room and closed the door behind him, leaving me alone to stew in my thoughts and feelings, I tormented myself in a grand way: *Just like Uncle Epitacio, I was going to die.* I was afraid. Monsters flew out of the closets, lively shadows sprang from the corners and the ceiling to grab me by my feet. Not one night, but many nights, until the tamale of my torment was cooked and someone I was not digested it.

Nearly forty years had passed and this tamale was reborn in Bad Homburg Park, but now I had it in hand and under control. I was the one who put that tamale in my mouth and gobbled it up. Now I knew what my last wish would be. I uttered "my last wish" and the memory of my grandmother's kitchen appeared in the romantics' beloved park, as if before a madeleine. Sure, I was going to die, yet knowing that, I felt no panic or fear of death. I wasn't locked up all alone, in a vast, dark room full of frightening, angry shadows, but in this beautiful park the romantics adored, as I adored them. They inhabited my memories; my treasures shone. That's not all. Now I knew a way to delay death's arrival: I am a person who writes, that's my trademark. We writers draw a line around death so it and its grinning skull cannot cross over. Saying the words "my last wish" didn't make me mortal, the way it had when I was a girl.

I was crossing Bad Homburg Park, as I said, floating on air and fascination until I reached the other side and the pedestrian street. I'd walked just a few steps when I saw on a table in front of the bookstore several volumes of classic Spanish writers for the very low price of one mark. It was a steal and a stroke of luck. I snapped up three works by Lope de Vega, although there were also Quevedo, *La Celestina*, and *El Conde Lucanor*. I went back across the divine park happier, and in better spirits, and reached my little cell with time left to look over my books. Since I only had ten minutes and since you read Lope de Vega on your knees (I was still floating with the emotion from the park), I sank my teeth into the prologue of *Caballero de Olmedo*, which, of course, was unattributed.

Suddenly, a paragraph gave me indigestion. I couldn't digest it; it was incomprehensible:

> The great authors of the Siglo de change *El caballero de Olmedo* to *Caballero de Olmedo* any time it appears Oro represent the peak of our letters.

You couldn't understand it at all. I retreated, pressed on, then returned, until I was able to untangle myself by adding parentheses in pencil: (change *The Horseman of Olmedo* to *Horseman of Olmedo* any time it appears), leaving: The great authors of the Golden Age represent . . .

The writer of the prologue realized that an error had been committed, that he had to strike out an excess article in the work's title. He confessed this to his computer, but failed to carry out the task. The error remained. His will to correct reverted to a tangle that made the prologue illegible. His confession did not redeem him.

I lost all confidence; I couldn't read a book published that way. I flipped past those pages searching for a credit but found none. My ride came. In silence we headed for Frankfurt; at the wheel was good Klaus, one of my hosts from the Liberaturpreis. I was thinking: "Here's my next novel, the life of Lope de Vega's German publisher, who edited the master for students studying Spanish, altering slightly here and there what he loves: the work of Lope de Vega." Thus *Thirty Years* was born, a novel that went down slightly different paths, moving to the imagined publisher's childhood and to the Mexican Caribbean. There in that car, because I'd crossed that park and found that book, because the writer had found no salvation in the end, I saw the character for the first time and caught a glimpse of the novel.

As night was falling on the way back to Bad Homburg, we saw a meteor shower. I couldn't face being locked up again with nothing to read (how could I trust a "tainted" editor), so I blurted out to Klaus and Susanne Lange, who had joined us, "Isn't there anything to do at night in Bad Homburg?"

Good Klaus, usually mute, broke into a story: yes, there was. In that very park was a casino nicknamed "the mother of Monaco." It had enjoyed enormous prestige and wealth until a kaiser, stirred by the tickling of his morals, decided that gambling was sinful, an unsuitable business, and closed the casino's doors. Thus he did the casinos in Monaco a favor; *their* doors opened. A few years later, the Bavarian monarchy lamented its economic losses and, setting scruples aside, reopened the casino in Bad Homburg. But it could no longer attract the star of chance and lost the claim to being number one. In any event, today it still has its prestige and legends. For instance, the story goes that Dostoyevsky found inspiration for *The Gambler* there and wrote his story in Bad Homburg, after losing his shirt. Although Dostoyevsky's biographer, Joseph Frank, does not support this story, I've set it down just the way Klaus told it.

Klaus invited us to the casino to observe third-world high rollers wasting prodigious amounts of money, with their enormous limousines waiting for them at the door. We went in, bet a round that Klaus squandered on us, no holds barred, drank champagne, and said good-bye.

The story about the birth of this novel tells, explains, some of the ingredients I use (or am used by) to write a novel:

1. Love aroused by reality (in this case by Bad Homburg Park)

2. Generosity of the real world (that gave me Lope de Vega's volumes for one mark — and with an error in the prologue!)

3. Awareness of the error

4. The desire to correct it, rewrite it, give it a frame that would tie it all together

5. Ignorance of an important territory we're most attracted to

6. Proximity to the passion for gambling

7. Fear of death

I begin with an account of a persimmon, motivated by my fear of death. This is conjured up in the novelistic exercise. With a sense of irony, Mexican cartoonist José Guadalupe Posada drew Death as an implacable skeleton, dressed in a ball gown, dancing. We novelists speak of death, keep it in mind. We talk about it in different words but always in praise of life, a confession of our passion for what is real, and, in so doing, we momentarily conjure it up. Our few or thousands of lines prolong our request for a last wish in which as we watch death we celebrate life. Ever since Scheherazade, we have written to delay death's arrival. We write to defy death: we are in the margins; it can't touch us. That other world we construct with our fables is totally impervious to death. If someone dies on our pages it's because *we*, not Death, determine it. We impersonate her, supplant her, steal cards out of her hand. We skin her or, to be precise, we steal her bones to make a shelter. We turn her into a tool, a resource.

The proximity of our passion for gambling, our need to tempt fate . . . You write a novel the way you stroke the great belly of possibilities. The novel can go this way . . . or that. The novelist rolls the dice. She is God and she is not. She's in control only up to a point. The dice rule. The author rolls them, but if she doesn't like the way they fall, she can gather them up and roll again. Again and again, until the number on the table is the lucky one. There are dice, there is chance, there is gambling. And there are powers greater than ourselves. That's how we impersonate death. As I write a novel, I feel like an archaeologist, as if the body of the book is already there and it is my job to uncover it without damaging it. It has a collective group of authors: my time, the times I live in, the story of my people. I don't invent the novel; it invents itself. It's up to me to make it legible, to work with the words so that if I'm lucky they tell a story.

Another element on my list is ignorance. I begin to work out a theme and look for characters because they have dark areas I can't fathom, because there's something I need to know, something I don't understand. They end up being something different from what I originally saw, what attracted me. For example, I wrote a novel about Cleopatra. I thought I wanted to set the record straight, to let what was lost have its say, to do battle with Aurelius's propagandists (Virgil, Cicero, and others). I never figured out why the subject had hooked me until the writing was over: because Cleopatra's image represents an iconic figure of love. She's the woman who destroys Caesar and Anthony; she is also the woman everyone desires. She is that mania in the flesh. And I needed to clean up my own house of love. I wrote to discover her and to discover myself; to rethink life through the eyes of the classic writers and their contemporaries; to rearrange love through them; to analyze why the memory of Cleopatra has been preserved from generation to generation with such passion and why I, of all women, had felt hooked by her. An unexpected hook: her character had never caught my attention, I had never joined that cult. In a way, Cleopatra-mania had seemed contemptible before, synonymous with a kind of vulgar flashiness. Suddenly I saw myself among the ranks of those I had scorned. (I'll come back to this.)

Getting back to that morning in Bad Homburg Park and "ignorance." I hadn't known that the famous casino in the park that I would admire and love in a subdued way existed. Because of my ignorance, I hurried out to find a book. Because I didn't know, I saw. Because I didn't know, I went searching around and found it. The novelist does that, too: he'll undertake the construction of his work, knowing full well he'll discover something unknown, a pearl, something he'll feel the need to rectify, to pay homage to, to critique, or to recount.

I write with a feeling of irritation. I must be truly engaged with the text or subject or character or feeling. Something lurking in the dark has to grab me. The "hook" or intellectual attraction is not enough. The thing that eludes me is the magnet. Something I don't know exists and that is not always the same. I'm not attracted to the pirates in *They're Cows, We're Pigs* just as I am not drawn to the Cleopatra of *Cleopatra Descends*, or to the Moctezuma in *Llanto*, or the little girls and the settings of my early novels. But in everything there is a common ingredient that gives birth to my relapsing spiritual-corporeal-intellectual obsessions. I search, through the anecdote, the text, the words. I search. I try to understand, to decipher.

Along with the text, my questions grow, the dark grows deeper, deeper. I get angry with myself. I rage. I write.

There is a constant battle. If "the dark" recedes, the text runs the risk of becoming smaller, of shrinking. But light is also essential. I have a clear idea of where I'm headed — the story line, the situations. Before I start a novel I figure out a plan, a map to follow, but there must be something very dark, darker than those vast nights of my childhood. At arm's length, just out of reach. This is not comfortable. As I've said, it irritates me, spurs me on, forces me on, and not with happy results. How annoying writing is! It's like playing at being Tantalus!

My irritation also feeds on the relationship I have with my characters. I don't choose characters who are admirable, or not admirable, in my eyes — or in other people's eyes. I feel my responsibility either to defend them or to support them and be on good terms with them. Those pirates, for example: their violence disgusted me as I wrote the book. It disgusted me, but I had to face it. With Cleopatra it was something else. I didn't want to buy into the affection her image stirs up or the hatred that she unleashed in her day. And on and on.

The next point: the desire to correct that error I mentioned earlier. I always long to point out an error and correct it. In some cases, to create a Utopia. In others, to create a hell, to adapt the facts to the surroundings that befit them. Errors of different magnitudes: historical injustices, for example. This mania marks the way I write. It may be the reason that all my work is "like" theater — not realism, not fantasy.

But, despite the ecstasy I felt, I tried to trick the real world, I tried to make an alternate reality in which the error I'd found didn't exist. I tried to underline the error, make it the protagonist, and give it a setting that obeyed it. I tried to take the "error" out of the error, so that it became something coherent, voluntary. I'd stumbled upon an error in an unsigned prologue. I imagined its author, I gave him will, I made him "perfect" (perfectly flawed), and bestowed upon him my grandmother's memories, the ones I imagined my grandmother had when I was young. I transported Lope de Vega's German publisher to the Tabasco of her childhood. What's more: the novel was written in a state of exaltation, taking long strides, as if it were running through Bad Homburg Park, fleeing death, begging for a last wish and then another. At night the grandmother tells the protagonist stories that like those of Scheherazade make the diurnal thread of time grow pale.

We novelists betray what we love most: reality. Why didn't I stop to describe this park's beauty and the relationship of those who loved it? Why didn't I describe my memory of my grandmother, her tamales, Epitacio? Why didn't I just throw the badly edited volume by Lope in the trash? I reiterate that my last wish is to see Bad Homburg Park again, some morning in autumn, yet as I was writing, I turned my back on it because I am a novelist. We are explorers, finders of treasures in the real world, but we long to betray reality. We point out the error in all that man makes and we remake it, in the process escaping the claws of death.

That's why I call my novel *Treinta años*, Daughter of the Park, the beautiful Bad Homburg Park [published in English as *Leaving Tabasco*]. It is also why I keep in mind another meaning of the word *park*: "The storage area for ammunition an army uses in time of war," because *Treinta años*, like *Llanto*, like *Antes*, like my other novels, is the daughter of the bullets I shoot — bang — to wound reality.

I started to write because I had nothing to cling to. As in fairy tales, everything happened when I turned fifteen. Some celebration! My mother died, the family was wrecked, and Mexico City had changed, too — the census reported three million people when I was born; now there are twenty million. It was my fate to watch it become a macropolis; in my adolescence that fact became crystal clear to me. My body was new, my adult body; the one I had known throughout my childhood was no longer mine; it had abandoned me. . . . Without a home or family, with a strange city, a strange body, what was I going to latch onto? Writing. I don't know why I chose to write, but I did, with almost mystical devotion. Maybe I chose to write because you didn't do that in my house, because I didn't know a single writer. Even though I had grown up surrounded by books, I didn't know that sort of people. It was a unique path, and I felt that it would give me a firm footing. I started to write to give myself backbone, a body, a city, a world, roots. My literary stammerings built me up in the midst of a world destroying itself, a world in flames. My writing made me whole among the ruins, the ruins of my childhood and my childhood memories, the ruins of family chaos, the ruins of the dizzying changes in a city that became a stranger to me at a time I thought myself incapable of taking its new measures.

At first, I wrote stories. Characters that didn't look like me, in situations that weren't mine. And yet they were. A very well dressed woman in high heels — a look I didn't present even on Sunday—crosses the street. A car runs over her. She's dead, but she crosses the street anyway, goes on her way as if nothing had happened. This is one story I remember. I discarded them all, or rather they discarded me — but let's not talk about that.

I started with a kind of writing that has grown more complex. I haven't yet learned to use words in a worldly, frivolous way. I don't know if I want to, although there are days when I would love to know how to write "second-hand," "opportunistic," "made-to-order" stories: today this happened, tomorrow that; to write with words that are "cool," up-to-date. "Up-to-date" is not in my vocabulary. Words carry their own time clock. I pursue them. They follow me. It's like a courtship. If that courtship is to go well, we — the words and I — must both be hot with passion. I believe words are always hot. But sometimes when I blaze with a perfumed, resplendent lust, words stick to me, they smell me and go crazy. Then other times they flee from me. I'm in love, and they're not. I smell bad to them. I try always to look my best for them so they'll desire me. I am careful when I give readings, careful with my routine, careful with my dreams; I apply myself, I always write, I read with greater attention and less desire to know how to innovate.

I say my words aren't up-to-date, but by that I don't mean they aren't mindful of the present. They are extremely mindful. In their way, they are pure present, the essence of the present. For example, as a result of September 11, 2001, the experience of living in the city where that horror took place and learning about the horrors that were unleashed thanks to President Bush, I wrote a novel. The main scene is the Battle of Lepanto, which took place in the seventeenth century when Spain defeated the Turks, and Cervantes lost a hand. There's a connection, I'm sure. The horror before the horror, the Christians against the Arabs, the holy wars, good men against Evil. . . . But it's not just that: a state, a milieu. I may be the only one who knows how to trace it back, to know that I was motivated by September 11, among other factors, to write *The Other Hand of Lepanto*, in which I pay homage to Cervantes's characters and world — in which the great author himself appears.

How is the ideal state of writing achieved? The state in which you write as if in a rapture, possessed? If I am in that state, the best and only thing to do is to follow a routine. A disciplined daily routine. But that's not enough. At least not in my case. I don't control the words. Of course I correct a thousand times on paper, on screen, on the blackboard of my mind. And of course I have a routine and discipline. But I don't rule over my words, neither do I delude myself that my inspiration and wishes run the show. When I write a poem it's as if the words came from very far away and I had the privilege of getting them to

a) "sing," making them pass through my mouth;

b) "dance," making them pass through my body;

c) "excrete," making them pass through my anus.

Because they need to come out, and that impulse is as strong as a bodily function. Although the three verbs I use are imprecise, because words "come out" passively, with no action, they are a verbalization with no verb. They speak to themselves. They want to be Beauty.

With this moment barely past, just set down on paper, I correct the words, correct and correct again, no longer in a state of feverish effervescence or exalted attraction, but with gentler and equally impassioned spirit. Though "passion" isn't the word for it — with a "need," like a compulsion. At the moment when the words "come out," I have the illusion that they are perfect, because there is a moment, before they solidify into grammatical entities, a moment when they are grinding around the earthen bowl of silence, before the ink dries, the ink that contains them, when they are pre-words, pure music, and they come bearing a *je ne sais quoi* that stutters on, bearing the weight of tradition and the lightness of the complete and most savage inventiveness.

I correct, trying to return them to that moment: to being pure light, filled with their nonverbal essence. When I write a novel . . . it's different up to a point. In both cases — prose, poetry — I'm not the absolute master; I don't hold the reins.

Am I clear? I want to be clear, because to me this process is very clear. I don't like to talk about it because I know it can sound like something it isn't: something anti-intellectual. This process is deeply intellectual and also entirely corporeal. It involves our nonverbal self. As if the word wanted to justify its existence apart from what doesn't fit into words, to rectify the path down which it has run and to remake itself, "regrammify," reverbalize itself.

And this process is clear for another reason: from the moment I start to correct, again and again, when I already know precisely how I want the words to sound, what I want the words to say, I am an artisan. I peck away, scrape, carve, polish, over and over. Like every artisan, I dream that the object I create will be understood, will be beautiful, will say something. So I carve and carve. In a sense I do govern, I do rule; I do consider myself the master. The years have taught me to enjoy this phase of the process. With equal intensity I am hopeless and enthralled. I keep on and on, and I want the process never to end, except for one reason: I'm worried the work won't be readable. I need to know that it is reaching the point of greatest understandability. I need a reader. And that's a problem for me, because I am a writer of the dark. Yet I don't want to write a line that has no meaning, that doesn't say something, that doesn't tell something, that isn't readable.

In a way, my childhood dream was a failure: words don't sustain me; they are not a spine, they are not my orthopedic device. The anxious longing to touch my words, to welcome them, to be able to use them, continues. In another way, my dream was a complete success: because I write, I have made a life for myself that I couldn't have found any other way. From being a social outcast, I became a woman with a profession, with children, a home, a man I love. Life has lavished riches upon me in every way, and I believe that's because I love and adore my profession. And not only when I hurried, nearly flew, through beautiful Bad Homburg Park, feeling that death will overtake me if I don't tell stories, if I don't hear a character coming, bearing his story so that I — could one be more privileged! — can tell it.

Translated by Pamela Carmell

Juan Villoro

(b. 1956)

The Phases of the Moon

Juan Villoro is among the most visible of contemporary Mexican writers. One sees his work in countless literary venues. Journalist, essayist, translator, short-story writer, educator, and novelist, he was for three years director of the excellent Sunday cultural supplement to *La Jornada*. He has been a contributor to numerous Mexican, German, and U.S. journals and newspapers, and that body of essays forms a respected overview of contemporary writers and writing.

In 2004 Villoro's novel *El testigo* won the coveted Premio Herralde de Novela. At the time of accepting the prize in Madrid, he commented on the "convulsive political change" taking place in Mexico following seventy years of one-party rule, adding that "in Mexico we have passed from perfect dictatorship to perfect caricature." Villoro credits three years in Barcelona for giving him sufficient distance to form an objective view of the political scene in his home country.

In addition to two other novels, Villoro has published a half-dozen books for children, a travel memoir, two collections of essays, one of chronicles, and six of short stories. It is this latter genre in which he may be most at home. He quotes Raymond Carver's humorous definition of the author who attempts that difficult form: "Writing short stories is a good fit for undisciplined authors unable to keep to a schedule."

In "The Phases of the Moon," with tongue-in-cheek good nature, Villoro offers his own views on the "miseries and marvels of being a short-story author."

———⊛———

The day man landed on the moon, I fell to Earth and broke a tooth. That afternoon, a bunch of friends from the neighborhood and I crowded around the TV to watch the epic drama in black and white, but the lunar landing was postponed so many times that we decided to go outside. We were devoting ourselves to the lesser epic of soccer until, in a burst of tragic inspiration, I tried a shot and fell face down on the asphalt. As I was testing gravity on Earth with my teeth, Neil Armstrong was jumping on the windless sands of the moon.

In the Middle Ages and during the Renaissance, parents employed a cruel, but memorable, technique: slapping their children to make them remember a certain scene. Pain seals memory. Thanks to my dramatic fall, I ended up in the chair of a lame dentist who didn't use anesthesia because his nurse fainted whenever she saw a needle. As he filed down my incisors, I suddenly understood the powers of the moon. I was twelve years old and belonged to the first generation able to comprehend that the Earth exists in order to be photographed from its natural satellite and that the only trace of humanity that can be seen from outer space was the Great Wall of China.

Some life experiences are solidified in memory by fear; others require imagination to find adequate accommodation. One of the advantages of writing consists of retroactively finding purpose in chance. Many years later, the distant afternoon when our father took us to discover ice becomes significant. Trying to find a clear picture of how I was first attracted to literature, I run across some sublunar experiences. In 1980 my first book, *La noche navegable* (*The Navigable Night*), appeared with a red moon on the cover, a sign that the journey would be presided over by the sphere that so closely controls oceans, women, insomniacs, and werewolves. At that time, I was working for Radio Educación, writing scripts for *El lado oscuro de la luna, la región desconocida de la música de rock* (*The Dark Side of the Moon, the unknown region of rock music*). In case there were any doubts about the attention I needed to pay to Selene's tasks, Abel Quezada celebrated the launching of *La noche navegable* by drawing a sailboat with two half-moons hanging from the mast.

In search of oracles, I read *The Great Wall of China* by Franz Kafka. The title alluded to the structure that can be seen from the moon, and the protagonist of the first story was the same age as me. "I was lucky that at twenty years of age, when I passed the final examination of the lowest school, the construction of the wall was just starting." My readings started to become organized like the bricks of the Great Wall. Kafka led me to Borges, and Borges to Monterroso.

One afternoon I opened the paper — like a sort of newsy *I Ching* — as I used to do in those days. That's how I found the announcement: Augusto Monterroso was giving a short-story workshop in the Alphonsine Chapel. Three students would be chosen and judged by an irreproachable jury. A few years before, I had gone to the tenth floor of the Chancellor's Tower in search of an ostensible workshop that Monterroso was supposed to be coordinating, only to find myself in a Kafkaesque mix-up. The maestro was as inaccessible as the Prague Castle. A rumor buzzed among the empty desks of the offices of Cultural Affairs: the maestro had resigned because he was fed up with the *tourists* in the story.

My second opportunity to be part of a workshop, with a contest and a year's stay in Alfonso Reyes's inexhaustible library behind me, seemed like something designed for the sedentary. Around that time, rock had produced a monument to kitsch: *Carmina Burana* in a version by Ray Manzarek, keyboardist with The Doors. Since I belong to one of the first generations to study that feat of engineering of ignorance known as CCH, I learned only those Greek and Latin etymologies that Marx includes in his famous phrases. Manzarek's notorious recording was useful, if for nothing else than to give me a Latin verse: *O Fortuna velut Luna*. Fortune changes as often as the moon. In other words, I was accepted into one of Monterroso's workshops.

It would be the height of vanity and gall to say I learned to write in a year of conversation dominated by Monterroso's irony. Like Cyrano de Bergerac, I thought I could travel to the moon without oxygen tanks. The maestro's lessons consisted of showing me just how far I was from my goal. The expedition would prove to be more arduous, and, if I could overcome the challenges, more rewarding. Monterroso's teaching method consists merely of dropping anecdotes with a calculated air of distraction. Like Lawrence Sterne, he turns digressions into the main point. His talks qualify him as one of the more frequent travelers to Cyrano's moon, so much so that at times he remains there, chatting on a first-name basis with Joyce, Quevedo, Gracián, and other favorites. Those classic literary soirées were designed not so much to correct the students' gaffes as to reveal the nature of the perfect story. Monterroso didn't waste any time trying to save us from ourselves; he showed us that life exists for the purpose of becoming a story, an essential value during those directionless years when I had placed all my hopes on a team that never won a championship and on girls who didn't seem to notice my tachycardia. Jorge Valdano says that César Luis Menotti gave him permission to dream. The phrase has the overblown pomposity of those who measure their destiny in ninety-minute sound bits, but it accurately describes the aim of all teaching. Monterroso gave me a belief system. The fragrance of sandalwood, the delicate bone structure of a hand, rain as an extension of lovers' fears, moonlight reflected in a pool of water, the barking of dogs in the night, freshly changed sheets, and the sound of the sea are all pretexts for writing stories. In any case, passion has a tendency to set priorities, even among those who practice several genres. Every time a spirited centaur visited the workshop, claiming to be writing a novel (something that was always four hundred pages long in those expansive days), Monterroso would remark: "Oh, you're training to write short stories!" No other kind of prose offers greater challenges for seekers of the instant spark. Can anything surpass the magic of an unusual ending that suddenly makes the previous ten pages fall perfectly into place? In this tense exchange of meanings, one superfluous word is an explosion, and the reader goes forward with the trepidation of someone deactivating dynamite. Besides, writing short stories suits those erratic types who can't adhere to schedules. According to Raymond Carver, it's the perfect occupation for a drunk who has only a few hours a day of lucidity, hates his family, and takes the car to a parking lot to write. And Graham Greene, toward the end of his life, chose the short narrative in order to be sure of finishing the text before he died. The domain of the "timesick," the short story is stimulated by the unfriendly parking meter that reads "About to Expire," and even by the death throes of its practitioners.

WHO'S BUYING THE CHAMPAGNE?

Coming out of Monterroso's workshop, I met a writer who was famous for his imaginative self-promotion techniques. With the troubled rictus of someone who's just bitten into an undercooked shrimp, he asked me, "You only write stories, don't you?" followed immediately by the unforgettable assertion, "Novels have more marketing possibilities." That novelist, the precursor of the ones who now write with optical lasers, convinced me of two things: He was a mercenary, and he was right. These days, short stories couldn't even pay F. Scott Fitzgerald's champagne bills. A realist, Monterroso insisted that we consider ourselves lifetime devotees.

In the quarter century that has elapsed since then, the situation has become even more precarious. In the seventies, short stories were like parrots: they weren't greatly sought after, but they could fit in anywhere. The art of Poe, Maupassant, and Chekhov survived without too many worries or defenders because, among other things, their active practitioners were called Jorge Luis Borges, Juan Carlos Onetti, Adolfo Bioy Casares, and Julio Cortázar.

Today, short-story writers are like those men who squat in the sun along Mexican highways, offering a product that very few people stop for: an iguana hanging by its tail. Editors today would rather adopt a child from East Timor than welcome a new short-story writer into their catalogues. With an agrarian take on culture, the short story has been relegated to harvest time: the World Soccer Championship heralds a volume of stories on that subject, and summertime permits alternating magazine photos of beauties in bikinis with brief texts, very useful for wiping suntan lotion off one's hands. It's no exaggeration to say that the opportunity for a young Juan Rulfo to publish *The Burning Plain* with an important publisher has been lost. Time and again, new writers presenting a volume of stories receive the same dictum: "Come back when you've got a novel." Some of the most important books of my generation are hard to find because they belong to an illusory genre: Fabio Morábito's *La lenta furia*, Francisco Hinojosa's *Cuentos hécticos*, Daniel Sada's *Registro de causantes*, Luis Humberto Crosthwaite's *Marcela y el rey*, and Emiliano Pérez Cruz's *Borracho no vale*.

Prizes make their recipients happy and demonstrate that all judgment is subjective. *La casa pierde* is as debatable as any other product of the imagination. Something I can indeed celebrate with certainty is the fact that the jury of the Premio Xavier Villaurrutia did pay attention to the short-story genre.

The book's title alludes to two different circumstances: the enormity of domestic failures and the power of chance. One of our first stories describes the drama of a man who cannot return home. This blend of uncontrollable wandering toward a familiar destination produced the grand saga now known as *The Odyssey*. No future technology will ever change that thrilling tension. Similarly, in the exterior space of the novel *Solaris*, the protagonist relieves his loneliness by clinging to the talisman of a civilization he abandoned light years before, and which has disappeared during his voyage: the key to his house. Nothing will cure us of this essential displacement: stories begin when the house loses.

A book about fortune must accept the fact that prizes depend on an expression that can be repeated a thousand times without losing its cotton-candy, carnival-like innocence: "lucky break." In 1980, when I published *La noche navegable*, my first publisher, Joaquín Díez Canedo, invited me to dinner at the Club Asturiano. We had just started the fifth course when a lottery ticket vendor interrupted us. Don Joaquín bought a bunch of tickets. "You have a better chance of winning with these than with literature," he told me, with the crooked smile of a man who has bitten down on many pipes.

Writing is a gambler's game, with no foreseeable reward other than the writing itself. Cervantes said it well: "Be patient and keep shuffling."

On January 20, 2000, the jury of the Premio Villaurrutia began deliberations minutes before a total eclipse of the full moon. In one of his early poems, Villaurrutia speaks of things that happen "beneath the secrecy of the moon." Any decision made under these circumstances is understandable. I lost a tooth for not watching the moon on TV, and I won a prize for not watching it in the sky. Thanks to the conspiratorial solidarity of my colleagues in the profession, today I can collect on the lottery ticket Joaquín Díez Canedo handed me twenty years ago. But no stroke of luck is final. Tonight the inconstant moon is out again.

Translated by Andrea G. Labinger

Ilan Stavans

(b. 1961)

Quest

Ilan Stavans is Lewis-Sebring Professor in Latin American and Latino Culture at Amherst College. As introduction, there is little one may add to quotes from the *New York Times*, "The czar of Latino literature in the United States," and the *Washington Post*, "Ilan Stavans has emerged as Latin America's liveliest and boldest critic and most innovative cultural enthusiast." They might also have added that Stavans is the most peripatetic, most omnivorous, and most wide-ranging, intellectually, of current Latinists. His prologues, essays, interviews, and "Conversations"—the title of a recent series of interviews conducted by Neal Sokol—cover subjects from Cervantes to García Marquéz, Sor Juana Inés de la Cruz to Isaac Bashevis Singer, and the conservator role of dictionaries to the prevalence of not only neologisms but also neolinguisms, the latter in his fascinating study of *Spanglish*, the mutual invasion, perversion, reinvigoration, and invention at the intersection of language where Spanish and English flow into one another. Stavans has said that Spanish speakers will all end up speaking Spanglish, and that while it is true that the currents rush more rapidly in that direction, it should not be ignored that Spanish, or *at least* Spanish as it is morphing into Spanglish, is more and more a presence in the everyday life of U.S. cities and towns with large Spanish-speaking populations.

The Essential Ilan Stavans contains seminal and negative as well as affirmative appraisals of such figures as Sandra Cisneros, Mario Vargas Llosa, and Subcomandante Marcos. To know Stavans, the reader may also consult *The Hispanic Condition*; *Art and Anger*; *The Riddle of Cantiflas*; *Latino USA: A Cartoon History*; *Growing Up Latino: Memories and Stories*; *Bandido*; a collection of stories, *The One-Handed Pianist*; and his autobiographical *On Borrowed Words: A Memoir of Language*. It is in the latter work that Stavans examines the ways that Spanish, Yiddish, Hebrew, and English shaped the words, and the worlds, of a child and young man who never felt at home in any culture, motivating his pilgrimage through multiple cultures to seek his place and his identity.

"It may be," Isaiah Berlin once said, "that no minority that has preserved its own cultural tradition or religious or racial characteristics can indefinitely tolerate the prospect of remaining a minority forever." Perhaps, but Mexican Jews thus did not exhibit signs of life. Content with their place on the margins, they refused to be disturbed. Or at least that's the impression I got. Shortly afterward, I found out about various kibbutzim near Jerusalem and, farther north, in Tiberias. A few friends from school were ready for Israel, too. [. . .] They made contacts, established routes, and offered advice. In Hebrew the whole enterprise was called Hakhsharah.

My first literary experiments — in Yiddish — belong to that time. In mid-1979, I staged a play of mine, *Genesis 2000*, loosely based on Antoine de Saint-Exupéry's *The Little Prince*, with a cast of twenty-five. It was favorably reviewed in the weekly *Der Shtime*. The public reaction mystified me. I was described as "a young Pirandello," "a promising voice," "a promising artist capable of digesting Brecht's lessons to the core." The problem: I had heard of Pirandello's *Six Characters in Search of an Author* but had not read it, let alone anything else by him; and likewise with Brecht. Before I attempted anything more in the theater, shouldn't I first find out what their legacy was about? [. . .]

I also wrote a pair of short stories in Yiddish, one of them a thriller that emulated the Hemingway of "The Killers," which I sent to *Die Goldene Keyt* in Israel, the only Yiddish literary magazine of some distinction published anywhere. I remember retyping them several times on a stolen typewriter with Hebrew characters, which I had borrowed from a friend and refused to return. (A new one would have to be imported from Israel and was thus too expensive.)

All this literary activity didn't make me feel happy. Yiddish wasn't truly mine. I asked the unavoidable question: Why write in Aleichem's language when its only readers are all in the geriatric ward? My voyage to Israel, I convinced myself, would offer some answers. It would provide room for self-knowledge.

MSP: Stavans did not find what he was seeking in Israel, so after six months on a kibbutz near Tiberias, a disenchantment with Orthodoxy, and an affair with an about-to-be-married female soldier, he decided that though he was enchanted with Hebrew, he was bored with Israel. He would continue his pilgrimage in Europe. In Toledo he met a young poet by the name of Fernando de Parcas with whom he explored Seville, along with the literary and religious history of Jews in Spain. Although Stavans was "infatuated" with the country, it was obviously not a place he could settle. "The past was there, but not the future." So it was back to Ciudad de Mexico.

I never saw de Parcas again, but it was thanks to his rediscovery of Judaism through poetry that I found a connection between the Spanish language and my Jewish self. Crossing from Gibraltar to Africa, I meditated on the development of Cervantes's tongue as a refuge for persecuted Sephardim.

El español was not a Jewish literary vehicle, at least not for those open about their Jewishness, even though the historian Américo Castro once argued that it was thanks to the Jews — especially those erudites in the court of Alfonso X, devoted to the craft of translation — that Spain came to find its soul in the Spanish language.

MSP: His return to Mexico was painful. It was the era of great political unrest, the time of the infamous "Noche de Tlatelolco," that Elena Poniatowska recorded in her testimonial account. "Action," he writes, "my only escape, I thought, was action." His activism inevitably led him to Cuba. However, that adventure, meant to "energize my political consciousness," had a negative effect, and he returned to Mexico once again, only to meet frustration and the persistent sense of alienation.

My reaction, yet again, was to burn my bridges, to abandon Mexico once and for all. But with Israel, Spain, and Cuba eliminated, where to go? Before long, I realized I needed to return to the Iberian Peninsula and the Middle East to exorcise their ghosts.

By then I was obsessed with literature. [. . .]

The magic of Spain — yes, I would become a young Hemingway in Madrid. The word was meant to be my home, but first I needed to appropriate it, to become its friend. [. . .]

If I had any talent as a writer, I needed to find out immediately. I found a job as a photographer's assistant that provided me with some money, and sold some belongings. I left for Spain without an itinerary but with a small green portable Olivetti, found myself a cheap room, and began to write.

Write, write, write . . . Not in Yiddish but in *español*, my own tongue. But words betrayed me. Did I really have something to say? A young Hemingway. Why? Didn't the world already have one? What was *my* place as a writer? A novel. I would produce a novel — the great Jewish–Latin American novel, one that could rival Saul Bellow's *Herzog*. I didn't know where to start, and so I crafted letters filled with longing and sadness . . . and I kept dreaming of Hoddie.

An author needs to know who and where his readers are, I repeatedly told myself. For whom was *I* writing? For my friends? But who were my friends? The comrades I had joined in public demonstrations? No, that facet of my life was over. Mexican Jews, perhaps? Truth is, they hardly read at all, and when they do, the last thing they want is a form of criticism of their *Weltanschauung*. I realized that "my second Spanish coming" was an extension of the first one. I was still as disoriented as ever, without a place to call home.

[. . .]

Depression. A shameful return. I had told friends and family that if I ever returned it would be with a full-length novel in hand. But I had nothing to show, only a vague belief that to complete what I had already started was the right step.

MSP: Stavans began to read voraciously on Judaism, Joseph Roth, Spinoza, Martin Buber, and Franz Rosenzweig. Along with them, Walter Benjamin and Gershom Scholem. In a conversation with a Jesuit priest, he discussed his plan to write a piece about a medieval Jewish mystic. The priest gave him a copy of Umberto Eco's *The Name of the Rose*, and in less than a month invited him to teach a course on Jewish philosophy.

It was then, while on the faculty as a Jewish teacher in a Catholic undergraduate school, that I began my first novel: *El error*, an esoteric tale of human mendacity set against the backdrop of an enclosed Hispanic university. My attempt was not only to explore the tension between dogma and *episteme* and use Franz Rosensweig as my secret model, but to examine the tension between Judaism and Christianity in the Hispanic orbit. [. . .]

The novel's fitting title was a statement of its quality. It was courteously rejected by the only publishing house I dared show it to: the small Editorial Artífice. It was dutifully destroyed soon after.

The owner of Editorial Artífice took me out to lunch at Café La Blanca, near the Palacio de Bellas Artes. After explaining the reasons for her rejection, she announced with the utmost tact that behind this failed experiment was a consummate author, who, for some unexplained reason, reminded her of Herman Melville, and in particular of his *Moby Dick*: a certain tendency toward the epic, an attempt to portray the clash between religions as a peremptory battle between moral systems, a portrait of a lone mystic as a stubborn "mariner who, as she looks out of her door's keyhole, sees the entire world before her. . . ." The connection surprised me: I had never read *Moby Dick* in full (I didn't even own a copy), nor was I able to grasp the link between my protagonist and Ahab, the captain of the *Pequod*, in his insane, revenge-driven mission to pursue the white whale. But the allusion flattered me. If it had been offered to make the negative news more palatable, its purpose was fulfilled, for, after a few days, once I recovered from the rejection, I told myself: You shall continue. The rejection is inconsequential. And you should read Melville. The more I thought about it, the better I understood that while drafting *El error* I had felt truly human, and its mere existence opened a door for me — yes, literature was the answer — my Promised Land, an authentic home, and a portable one at that, which I was able to carry around with me. Henry Thoreau once wrote, "The art of life . . . is, not having anything to do, to do something." Herein, I concluded, lay the true utopia: finding raison d'être, inventing your own private homeland.

Translated by Margaret Sayers Peden

Pedro Ángel Palou, Eloy Urroz, Ignacio Padilla, Ricardo Chávez Castañeda, & Jorge Volpi
Crack *Manifesto*

In 1996 a group of young, urban writers—all very close in age—expressed their views in a manifesto written in five voices. This credo was published that same year in a little magazine that quickly disappeared. It appeared later in the October 2000 issue of *Lateral*, a journal that has served as a major voice for *Crack* writers.

Literary movements in Mexico, as elsewhere, are usually loosely defined by generation, by gender, by reaction against an earlier style of writing, or by a combination of factors similar to those that united the *Contemporáneos* group in Mexico during the twenties and thirties: sexual orientation and a general agreement that the literature produced during the years of the dictatorship of Porfirio Díaz at the turn of the century, and then during the twenty years of the Mexican Revolution, had too long rejected idealism and universality and placed too much emphasis on realism and nationalism. In their expressed intent to turn their eyes away from Mexico and toward Europe, *Crack* bears some resemblance to those *Contemporáneos*.

The *Crack* went further than most movements, however, in that it stated its credo publicly, and then each member of the group did, in fact, write a novel using the specific guidelines of their manifesto: *Si volviesen sus majestades,* by Iganacio Padilla; *Memoria de los días,* by Pedro Ángel Palou; *La conspiración idiota,* by Ricardo Chávez Casteñeda; *Las rémoras,* by Eloy Urroz; and *El temperamento melancólico,* by Jorge Vopi. These works met with varying success, but *Crack's* founders have continued to publish, some more prolifically than others. It is difficult to think of such a structured and openly publicized approach to writing since the Surrealist manifesto of André Breton.

Crack, it should be made clear, does not refer to the drug, but to the sound of "rupture."

———————

Pedro Ángel Palou
(b. 1966)
I. The Crack Fair (A Guide)

I believe it was Italo Calvino in *Six Proposals for the Next Millennium* who most accurately described the challenges presented to the *Crack* novels. In those pages, Calvino proposed a necessary consideration for these times, when literature, and above all, narrative, finds its potential readership displaced by entertainment technology: video games, mass media, and, recently, for those who can afford them, virtual reality games in which — oh, paradoxes of development! — an individual equipped with a state-of-the-art helmet and a sensor-equipped glove can see, hear, and even feel the adventures brought to him by a compact disk.

How, then, can the narrator compete, with his meager resources for winning over readers who are lost in this vast world of few shadows? Calvino, ahead of his time, knew the answer: by using the most ancient weapons of the oldest profession (remarks about prostitution notwithstanding) in the world:

Lightness. Calvino considers this literary virtue, suggesting that works like *Romeo and Juliet* or *The Decameron* or even *Don Quixote* constructed their powerful narrative machinery while maintaining a strange lightness. Or rather: an apparent simplicity. By using this strategy, it became easier to deal with a terrible moral message. An incisive vision and an acerbic social criticism are subordinated to a fresh, buoyant sense of humor that is, however, not devoid of the most piercing sarcasm. Chesterton said that humor in literature should produce hilarity while freezing the smile in a reflective rictus that halts time and exhumes the mirror.

OUR FIRST ATTRACTION AT THE CRACK FAIR: THE FUN HOUSE

Speed. Communication theorists have known for some time that the information implosion is linked to the deflation of meaning. The Persian Gulf War, the first ever to be transmitted by satellite, taught us this. We didn't really learn anything, yet we thought we saw and understood everything. Nevertheless, we cannot deny that what first amazed us was its terrifying coldness. If the world was swayed (and the verb is used deliberately) at the beginning of the last century with the sinking of the *Titanic,* today the tragedies of the war in Sarajevo neither impact nor move us: they inform us.

SECOND ATTRACTION: THE ROLLER COASTER

Multiplicity. Don Quixote is perhaps the multiple work *par excellence* in the history of literature. *Gargantua* treads close on its heels, and *Tristram Shandy* carries its suitcase. Today, although to say so is to belabor the obvious, reality hurls itself at us in multiple forms, reveals itself to us as many sided, eternal. We need books in which a total world opens up before the reader and captures him. We have used that same verb elsewhere, but here the strategy is different. It isn't a question of vertigo, but rather of the superimposition of worlds. To employ all the metaphorical potential of the literary text in order to remind ourselves: "Here you are, discover yourselves."

THIRD ATTRACTION AT THE CRACK FAIR: THE HALL OF MIRRORS

Visibility. The ultimate virtue of prose: its crystalline texture. None other than Flaubert expressed it as follows: "What a damned business prose is!

One never stops correcting. A good piece of prose must be as rhythmic and musical as good verse." Not just idle formalism, but a quest for the intensity of form, the profound use of the magnificent virtues of the Spanish language and its multiple meanings.

FOURTH ATTRACTION AT THE FAIR: THE CRYSTAL BALL

Exactness. Calvino subtly warned us to isolate the values we have been discussing. And it is in this last section where we can demonstrate how there can be no exactness without precision, and how lightness is impossible without vertigo, transparency, and speed. All good prose is *exact*. Even more important, balanced. The hoary obsession with content and form is irrelevant when a literary work faithfully seeks exactness. Conan Doyle, for whom effect was everything, knew this. In order to achieve exactness, one must resort to all the rest. But perhaps the greatest lesson of Calvino's proposal is to make us understand that the exactness of a literary work is impossible if it doesn't come naturally, without effort. Picasso *dixit*: "Inspiration exists, but it has to catch you working." What do we mean? Agility, the power to describe (and describing is observing with the intention of making things interesting, as Flaubert desired, but it also means selecting those small, great things that not only make up a part of life, but which are life itself), as well as that ingredient that allows the reader to continue reading nonstop, with growing curiosity. Here one can see the importance that exactness, implied by using the precise word at the right moment, must hold for the late-twentieth-century narrator.

And here we come to our last attraction:

THE SHOOTING GALLERY

Consistency. Italo Calvino planned to write this section relying solely on an analysis of one of Melville's most beautiful texts, *Bartleby, the Scrivener.* This odd character, an employee in a law office, gradually refuses to participate in existence, repeating the phrase, "I would prefer not to." At the end of the tale, Bartleby is locked up and dies repeating this sentence, even refusing to eat.

Consistent with its life plan and its future, the *Crack* novel fancies itself a sort of renewal: from the last traditional attraction, it revisits the *Crack* fair from the beginning, with the same will to capsize, as revealed in the following tetralogy:

1. *Crack* novels are not small, digestible texts. They are, rather, a barbecue of chewy cuts: let others write steaks and meatballs. In contrast to the frivolity of the disposable and ephemeral, *Crack* novels offer a multiplicity of voices and the creation of autonomous worlds. No mean feat. First commandment: "Thou shalt love Proust above all others."

2. *Crack* novels are born not of certainty, mother of all creative annihilation, but rather of doubt, elder sister of knowledge. Thus, there is not one single type of *Crack* novel, but many; there is not one prophet, but many. Each novelist discovers his own pedigree and displays it with pride. Descendants of champions, *Crack* novels run all risks. Their art consists more of being inconclusive than of concluding. Second commandment: "Thou shalt not covet thy neighbor's novel."

3. *Crack* novels are ageless. They are not *Bildungsroman*, and they repudiate Pellicer's statement: "I am aged, and the world was born with me." They are not, therefore, their authors' first novels, where the temptations of autobiography, first love, and the settling of family debts weigh above all else. If the novelist's most valued possession is freedom of imagination, these novels exaggerate that fact by seeking the continuous multiplication of their narrators. Nothing is easier for a writer than to write about himself, nothing more tedious than a writer's life. Third commandment: "Thou shalt honor schizophrenia and thou shalt hear other voices; let them speak in thy pages."

4. *Crack* novels are not optimistic, sunny, pleasant, novels; they know, as did Joseph Conrad, that being hopeful in the artistic sense doesn't necessarily imply believing in the goodness of the world. Rather, they seek a better world, knowing, perhaps, that in some unknown place, such a fiction might occur. *Crack* novels are not written in that new Esperanto, the standardized language of television. A festival of language, and — why not? — a new Baroque: of syntax, of vocabulary, of wordplay. Fourth commandment: "Thou shalt not participate in any group that would have thee as a member."

Eloy Urroz
(b. 1967)

II. The Genealogy of Crack

In his famous essay, *Mexico in Its Novel*, North American critic John S. Brushwood insisted that Agustín Yáñez established the tradition of the "profound novel" in 1947 with the publication of *The Edge of the Storm*. Subsequently, in 1955, and within the same tradition, *Pedro Páramo* appeared, of which Brushwood said: "Quite naturally, some readers object to the difficult access to the novel, and some prefer to reject it rather than work for what it says. I can sympathize with the reluctance to participate so actively, but it seems to me that the result is worth the effort." What doesn't fail to call one's attention here is, first of all, the accurate use of the adjective "profound" to refer to a tradition or an earnest chain of novels and novelists that, in their day, did indeed "profoundly" understand creative work as the most genuine expression of an artist dedicated to his craft.

When Brushwood speaks, for example, of "difficult access" to certain books, *Crack* authors immediately think of the novel that makes "demands," not "concessions," "demands" that are ultimately "worth the effort" and "concessions" that in the long run serve only to further weaken the landscape of our narrative and to discourage serious readers. The dilemma, then, of this group of *Crack* novels is that they attempt to cultivate what Julio Cortázar called "active participation" in their readers at a time when a loathsome inarticulateness is what sells and what readers devour.

Thus, the genealogy of *Crack* continues to take shape. *Crack* clears the undergrowth and fixes the boundaries for those books to which it feels indebted and for those books whose anathema or inquisitor it considers itself to be: many are the novels that will be tossed into the bonfire without mercy and without ado.

Along with this tradition that reaches its splendor in Yáñez and Rulfo, as we have already stated, *Crack* novelists revere those few works known as *Farabeuf, Los días terrenales (Days on Earth), La obediencia nocturna (Nocturnal Obedience), José Trigo, The Death of Artemio Cruz*, and a few others. But what has happened since then? What are the exemplary works of our literature, or, at least, which tales are those that we, authors born in the sixties, can use today to slake our thirst or as a model worthy of destroying and thereupon usurping? They don't exist: they have died of anemia and self-complacency. Risk-taking and the desire for renovation have languished. A decades-old lacuna muddies the realm of letters with its absence, whether it be the fault of novelists who don't write, or worse yet, writers who cannot call themselves novelists. To be frank, there are few exceptions, and their novels are no better than good; good, I repeat, as in "proper," devoid of any shock value that might offend an insipid social contract and insipid literary norms.

The earnest chain of legitimately "profound" novels, therefore, suffered a terrible blow when large publishing houses began to vacillate a few years ago, preferring to sell the public phony "profound" titles, literary fakes, thus "bait-switching" readers on a grand scale and, in the process, deactivating the urgent need for reader involvement produced by texts such as *Hopscotch*, *A Brief Life*, or *One Hundred Years of Solitude*. Today this phenomenon has become so threatening and evident that one can only describe it as lamentable. Nonetheless, we *Crack* novelists dream that in some part of our literary republic there exists a group of readers who are bored, fed up, sated with so many concessions and so much complacency. They, you, can no longer be fooled. The concessions, I repeat, unnerve them and only lead them to believe that their own capabilities are being underestimated.

It is this group of individuals, you, our readers — just a few thousand of you, alas — that the *Crack* novels attempt to reach, pursuing, I repeat, that genealogy that our national culture has forged ever since the days of the Contemporáneos Group (or perhaps a bit earlier) whenever it has attempted to run real formal and aesthetic risks. There is no break, then, but rather continuity. And if there has been a sort of break, it has been only with the deadwood, today's noxious Gerber baby pap, that literary "formula-for-the-naïve," the cynically superficial, dishonest novel. At any rate, the fact is that anything my colleagues or I might say here doesn't matter. In the end, the *Crack* novels will speak for themselves. There they are. They're called: *El temperamento meláncolico* (*The Melancholy Temperament*), *Memoria de los días* (*Memory of Days*), *Si volviesen sus majestades* (*If Their Majesties Return*), *La consipración idiota* (*The Idiots' Conspiracy*), and *Las rémoras* (*The Remoras*). If they share any common denominator, I believe it's risk — aesthetic risk, formal risk, the risk always implicit in the desire to renovate a genre (in this case, the novel), and the risk involved in perpetuating what is most profound and arduous, summarily eliminating all that is superfluous or dishonest. It's time to stop underestimating you. In the words of the poet Gerardo Deniz, which have become my watchwords: "Time does not heal. Time verifies." Let us hope time will give the *Crack* novels the last word.

Ignacio Padilla
(b. 1968)
III. A Pocket Septet

1. FATIGUE AND HOPELESSNESS

If Pessoa, by himself, was able to create an entire generation in the dictatorial, literary wasteland of Lisbon, it was, ideas notwithstanding, due to fatigue. One morning after a restless sleep, Álvaro de Campos awoke to write, "Because I hear, I see. I confess: it's fatigue." And from his insomnia, great poetry was born. Similarly, I believe that all breaks with the past, from the most routine ravings to the cruelest and most radical revolutions, arise not from ideologies, but from fatigue. That's why it's pointless to look for conclusive definitions or theories here. Perhaps only a few strange "isms" would appear, more in jest than as manifesto. And that would be a mere reaction to exhaustion, weariness at the notion that our great Latin American literature and that dubious magical realism have become the tragic parlor tricks of our letters, the weariness of those jingoistic speeches that for so long tried to make us believe that Rivapalacio was a better writer than his contemporary, Poe, as if proximity and quality were one and the same; weariness from writing badly in order to be read more widely, but not better; weariness from the obligation to be *engagé*; weariness from letters that buzz, like flies, around their own corpses. From that exhaustion comes a general death certificate, not just literary, but circumstantial as well. I'm not talking about phony or fly-by-night pessimism or existentialism. Perhaps we can still benefit from the fact that the spirit of comedy, laughter, and caricature will become alternatives.

2. OF THE ABSENT STRUGGLE
AND OTHER NEGATIVE DEFINITIONS

The Sicilian expression, "generation without a struggle," isn't as meaningless as some think. It contains irony for those readers of Ortega y Gasset who recognize struggle as one of the characteristics he listed as defining a generation.

In effect, the lack of struggle is one of the few elements that unite us, like it or not. And if something is happening with the *Crack* novels, it isn't a literary movement but rather, simply and plainly, an attitude. The only proposal is the lack of a proposal. We will leave it to the more righteous to develop one at the proper time, as they no doubt will. This is not the only definition in negative discourse; it is not just the lack of struggle, as if we were theologians defining God or hell. We can say only that, more than "being something," *Crack* novels "are not many things." They are everything and nothing, that expression with which Borges accurately defined Shakespeare. Sometimes definitions kill mystery, and a literature without mystery doesn't deserve to be written.

3. CREATIONISM FOR ESCHATOLOGY

Let us not be deceived: *Crack* novels, while certainly apocalyptic, lack eschatological originality. It would be unfair to ascribe this tendency to them, unfair to a long tradition that, of course, is not exactly Mexican. And if this isn't proof enough, the end of ideologies and the fall of the Berlin Wall greatly preceded literature in this regard; long ago we were left the legacy of a world made of suffixes, merely suffixes that we add, sometimes in earnest and almost always as a desperate joke, to whatever already existed, to what already was. Beckett long ago predicted such a situation for the genre, not in *Godot*, but in his *Endgame*. Like Hamm and Clov, we don't write from the Apocalypse, which is ancient, but rather from a world beyond the end. If there seems to be a Creationist zeal in these novels, not in the literal sense of Huidobro, but in the broader interpretation of Faulkner, Onetti, Rulfo, and so many others, it is because we consider it necessary to construct that grotesque cosmos in order to have a greater, more plausible, right to destroy it. And once destroyed, only then will the *Crack* novels begin to appear within the empire of chaos.

4. Chronotype Zero,
or Toward an Aesthetic of Dislocation

This world beyond the world does not aspire to prophesy or symbolize anything. Perhaps it sometimes uses tricks to achieve a distancing effect in homage to Brecht and Kafka, a nod to the grotesque or caricatural paraphrases. In reality, what Crack novels seek to achieve are stories whose chronotype, in Bakhtinian terms, is zero: nonplace and nontime, all times and places, and none. From the comic tradition, we have taken what the revisers of *Amadís of Gaul* did, by accident and more than half a millennium ago, and what the Austrian Ransmayr did only five years ago, by placing his Publius Ovidius Naso before a bouquet of microphones. Dislocation in these *Crack* novels will be, in the long run, simply the imitation of a crazed, dislocated reality, the product of a world whose mass-mediazation has brought it to the end of a century that is truncated in both time and place, broken by an excess of ligaments.

5. Nimbus and Word

It is left to the *Crack* novel, therefore, to renew language from within itself, that is, by nourishing it from its most ancient ashes. Let others, those who have faith, treat language with factional argot or with the discourse of Rock, which already sounds old-fashioned. There are still more books to be written. There is cloth to be cut from paremiology, from the rhapsodist's orality, from archaisms and atavistic language, oral tradition and folklore, the rhetoric of troubadours and clerics. These resources, at least, have demonstrated a greater resistance to time, and although this alchemy may appear to be more difficult, its results are richer.

6. In Praise of Monsters

No one writes novels anymore, or rather, no one writes "total" novels anymore. But, I ask myself, novels for whom? Total for whom? Are they even being written? It would be better to speak of supreme novels and of names like Cervantes, Sterne, Rabelais, and Dante, together with all those who openly followed them. It's a question of organisms that shouldn't scare us away with their enormity, of which we shouldn't deprive ourselves for fear of their monstrousness.

More arrogant, it seems to me, is the author who would distance himself from those giants, using the questionable pretext of his incapacity and saying that those — we — who openly take on the monsters should stumble along with them. Literature that denies its tradition cannot and must not develop in it. No monster denies its shadow. Novel or antinovel, mirror reflecting mirror: this is the only possible way to achieve rupture with dignified continuity.

It's pointless to shake a jar of ticks. This is a game, like everything worthwhile in literature. The word is one and the same; the novel, no matter what they say, has been with us always and will continue. By breaking it, it prevails. In effect, if there's nothing new under the sun, it's because the old matters when creating the new.

Ricardo Chávez Castañeda
(b. 1961)

IV. The Risks of Form. Structure of the Crack Novels

Clichés such as "the pages speak to us" or "the book stands on its own" become relevant when evaluating an aesthetic proposal. If a manifesto is, in the best of cases, a map for outlining what should be obvious with even a fleeting look at common denominators, the works themselves are the real testimonials of commitment to a position and a declaration.

The five *Crack* novels are precisely the place where one should look for whatever there may be of pact, potential soul, and ambition, of whatever may be staked on a — let's call it "profound" — literature at this moment and by these writers.

What is most extraordinary is their coincidence. The novels were developed without a common directive. If they later became grouped together, it was due less to determination than to a shared destiny in the ever-voluble medium of publishing houses, and, more important, to a confluence of postulates, promises, and perhaps — why not? — lack of realized objectives.

Expositions like this one only add to our astonishment: until now, flowing into the episodic accidents of the times had been the only commonality among us: authors born at the beginning of the sixties.

In short, we are joined together today by a shared verdict, if it is understood that the novels already are — for better or for worse — a boundary and a declaration of process. From this point on, it is merely a question of exploring the choice that was made and extracting every last consequence of that choice.

What are the terms of the agreement? What is the pledge?

The books are the only place where one can look for the answers; however, first we can bring out the map that minimizes all declarations of principles in order to facilitate defense as well as attack.

Crack novels essentially share the notions of risk, challenge, rigor, and that overarching will that has generated so many mistaken ideas. *Si volviesen sus majestades*, *Memoria de los días*, *La conspiración idiota*, *Las rémoras*, and *El temperamento melancólico* reject any established, mass formula. They run the risk of being considered tentative efforts. One could accuse them of being incomplete, although not of lacking ambition to explore the novelistic genre to the maximum with weighty, complex themes and their corresponding syntactical, lexical, and stylistic systems, using the necessary polyphony, "baroquisms," and experimentation, with a rigor devoid of pretexts and complacency.

Thus, while an entire sect assumes the responsibility of narrating the end of the world in *Memoria de los días*, it is the voices of the actors bursting forth in the movie filmed in *El temperamento melancólico* that tell us of the infinite hubris of a director who thinks of himself as God. At the other extreme, *Si volviesen sus majestades* mounts a chaos of inner stories, like jewels, within the apparent order of its main narrative, similar to the manner in which three short Cervantine novellas interrupt Ricardo's principal voyage to *Las rémoras*. And, in a final tour de force, *La conspiración idiota* proposes to spell out the secret language of children with a vocabulary as original as the one sputtered by our buffoon in *Si volviesen sus majestades*.

In the *Crack* novels you will find, then, the span of the project but also its limits, its triumphs but also its absurdities. Nothing is slanted, nothing altered, because any worthwhile project contains only extremes, as high and as low as the ascent or the fall may require.

Such a book is necessarily weighty and harsh for its readers. The *Crack* novel demands, but it also offers. It prides itself on reciprocity: the more one seeks, the more one will receive, with the assurance that the iceberg has always been there to settle any debt.

Precision is required here. Unlike those voracious novel-worlds that aspire to everything and reveal everything, those books that regard themselves at once as scientific, philosophical, enigmatic, et cetera, and which, like life itself, discard as much as they gird on without ever changing, the all-encompassing *Crack* novels generate their own universe, greater or smaller as the case demands, yet intact, hermetic, and precise.

The *Crack* books created their own code, and they have taken it to its ultimate extreme. They are egocentric universes, almost mathematical in their construction and foundations, unconditional in their urgency to understand realities chosen from all perspectives, which in literature translates into a multiplicity of registers and interpretations; there is no point that doesn't tangle or loop, like a net that is a combination of knots and holes.

In short, this is nothing new. At most, it unearths a forgotten aesthetic in Mexican literature. We have chosen ascendancy and just one of a thousand possible paths. The proposition, therefore, has been made, written, and now published because any dialogue concerning a literary proposal is brought to life through the books: "The pages speak to us"; "The books stand on their own."

Crack is ready to do it.

Jorge Volpi
(b. 1968)

V. What Became of the End of the World?

The bizarre members of the Church of the Peace of Our Lord who appear in *Memoria de los días* feverishly march toward Los Angeles in search of converts and, though they may not know it, toward the destruction of their world. The diverse court of characters — one more eccentric than the other — the scribe, the wrestler priest, the reincarnation of the Virgin, all variants of a perverse narrative lottery — traverse the world trying to explain to skeptics that the universe is about to come to an end, just as Carl Gustav Gruber, the acclaimed film director in *El temperamento melancólico,* does. Some people listen to them, a few follow them, but most ridicule or condemn them. It will take a crazed North American, a David Koresh–like figure, to unleash a massacre among the faithful.

Scientists, like critics, believe they have the final word: Judgment Day turns out to be a hoax; objectively, nothing has changed. What they don't realize, what they are incapable of understanding, is that the fires in Los Angeles are, in reality, the long-announced hecatomb. Because they lack the fortitude and bravery to realize, paraphrasing Nietzsche, that the end of days does not occur beyond the world but, rather, within the human heart. More than a decimal superstition or a market necessity, the end of the world presupposes a particular spiritual condition; what matters least is external destruction, compared with internal collapse, with that state of anguish that precedes our personal Judgment Day.

In the same way, a millenary coincidence has caused other pilgrims to set out for these lands as well: Ricardo and Elías, a pair of ridiculous Siamese twins, who have invented each other without realizing it, advance along the road that goes from La Paz to the California border, en route to that same Babel of immigrants, and from there, perhaps, to Alaska. In a multiple world in which stories within stories abound, as in *Si volviesen sus majestades*, the aesthetic of Escher or Borges seems to reach its ultimate extreme in *Las rémoras*, the name of the novel as well as that of the fishing village where that rite of reunification takes place. We are divided, or multiple, beings; who can deny it? The radical factor here is that only writing can reintegrate us with our ghosts, making it possible for the imaginary friends of our adolescence to appear like real beings or, worse yet, like the authors of our days. Hidden, the end of days here becomes the beginning of Utopia, the beginning of a new world. United at last, Elías and Ricardo, at once creator and creation, stop in the middle of the desert, and, urinating by the side of the road, contemplate the unfathomable space of the End, the beginning of the universe, that still lies before them.

What happens with the gang of elderly adolescents who undertake *La conspiración idiota* is no different. A few adults determine to recall their childhood adventures, especially the destiny of Paliuca, the strangest one of all, who suddenly, many years earlier, decided he had to be good. Thus, they meet randomly, trying to unravel the minor mystery that joins them to Paliuca. However, the apparent clarity of the plot conceals a secret: truth does not exist; all that matters is the internal experiences of the characters, who can barely explain to us who they are. The style and syntactical texture of the sentences, as in the Seneschal's awkward language in *Si volviesen sus majestades*, subvert conventions in order to demonstrate to us again that the end of the world happened long ago, in that unnamed, abstruse region that separates innocence from cruelty, childhood from maturity.

It is also an unlikely coincidence that the faithful Seneschal of the shimmering kingdom abandoned by Their Majesties eternally dreams of traveling to the land of Kalifornia, with a "k," since in that world, books have disappeared, leaving society's obsession with cinema as a substitute. But so it is: Kalifornia appears as a recurring topos of fin de siècle passion, a space for massacre or flight. Yet, unlike his counterparts in *Memoria de los días* or *Las rémoras*, the Seneschal will never manage to reach his dream. Because — alas! — the end of the world is the Seneschal himself. His murky figure, his exquisite sadomasochism with the Buffoon, and his lingua franca that evokes, or rather subverts, the "scoundrel Avellaneda's" Castilian, contain the entire universe, Their Absent Majesties and all, and therefore — horror of horrors — its fruitful destruction. The end of the world is also schizophrenia, a fantasy, a hypochondriacal Big Crunch. The conclusion should surprise no one: the Seneschal has done nothing other than search for his identity through language and delirium like an "oligophrenic" Rumpelstiltskin, for that same identity that all the *Crack* characters might well possess: from this day forward, their name shall be Chaos.

For his part, Carl Gustav Gruber, the famous, nonexistent, German film director, shares with Elías, the scribe of *Las rémoras*, and with Amado Nervo, the Golden Pen of *Memoria de los días*, a privileged characteristic: an artist on the surface, he turns everything his hands touch to dust. Is not sterility, without going any farther, the real end of the world? Is mediocrity not oblivion? Gruber obsessively makes his last film: he has cancer and, what's worse, he can infect his actors with it through his words, through his hideous melancholy temperament. With that same zeal for perfection, he infects his following of last men, another guild, another fraternity as in *La conspiración idiota,* but one that is distinguished by its excessive malleability. Like Gruber, everyone is — or thinks he is — an artist. All of them are prepared to sell their souls for that noble cause. And they all pay the price.

The end of the world might be believed in and prophesied, as *Memoria de los días*; it may be reachable by ferry or automobile, as in *Las rémoras*; it may be recollected and reconstructed in childhood and the past, as in *La conspiración idiota*; it may be triggered in the individual himself, leading to madness, as in *Si volviesen sus majestades*; and it may also be granted to others, like the notorious Pandora's Box, as in *El temperamento melancólico*. Regardless, in none of these cases can anyone escape this final illness, this Fifth Horseman, this plague, and this diversion: this ultimate state of the heart.

MEXICO CITY, AUGUST 7, 1996

Translated by Andrea G. Labinger

Ignacio Padilla

(b. 1968)

Crack in Three and a Half Chapters

In the same issue of *Lateral* in which the *Crack* manifesto was published, Ignacio Padilla contributed a history of the group, "Crack in Three and a Half Chapters." Since the declaration of their credo, *Crack* writers have enjoyed critical and popular successes. Jorge Volpi won international acclaim for his novel *In Search of Klingsor*; Ricardo Chávez Castañeda has garnered a bouquet of prizes for short story: the Premio Borges de Cuento, Premio Latinoamericano de Cuento, and Premio Aresti de Cuento; and Padilla himself has an impressive list of *galardones*, among them, the Premio Nacional de Ensayo Literario—twice—and the Premio Primavera de Novela. All in all, a notable affirmation of the group's talents and literary acumen.

In the prologue to *La catedral de los ahogados* (Cathedral of the Drowned), Padilla offers one scenario for the genesis of a novel.

"It was under those circumstances that Orlando conceived a story. He would write a grotesque tale in a world subjected to his laws and his demons. He himself would thus become the god of a new island. He would decide when to end it and when to start it again. Perhaps in this way, he thought, the first island would cease to torture him with its incomparable beauty, and he would at last be able to sleep. It should be easy: wait for the tide to come in, bide his time until the story was erased, and then write a new version. Only the arbiter of nature could make bearable the sleeplessness that invited him every minute to take his own life. And so it was that Orlando went back to the beach, broke off a twig from a plum tree, and with it began to write the stories of his insomnia in the sand."

The novel that followed won the Premio Nacional Juan Rulfo.

—— ✦ ——

I'm now pleased, rather than annoyed, by the erroneous — and not infrequent — application of the term *Crack* to an entire generation of Latin American writers born in the sixties. Just as in poetry, there are some providential mistakes we wish were true. I know, however, that many of my highly talented contemporaries don't completely or even partially share — and have no reason to — the aesthetic proposals made by *Crack*. It is in order to do justice to these authors that I've now decided to present this brief chronology of what I daresay can be considered a literary group embedded, to its great fortune, in this current, vigorous generation of Latin American narrators.

It's partially true that we members of the *Crack* Group can be measured to a certain extent by the stick imposed on us by a good number of generational classifications, but at the same time I think it's fair to say that this group is primarily characterized by something many critics today would consider anti-intellectual and even a bit suspicious: our literary friendship. Any chronology of *Crack* necessarily involves the difficult task of tracing, step-by-step, the story of certain close bonds of friendship that, while not necessarily or invariably literary, do adhere closely to the fortunate concurrence of souls previously dispersed through books. With a few inevitable exceptions, the six *Crack* members were all born in the second half of the sixties — that is, along with *One Hundred Years of Solitude* and in close proximity to the chaos of 1968. We are inveterate travelers, accidental academics, storytellers by vocation, and strict urbanites. Nearly all of us were born in the largest city in the world; we witnessed what came to be known as the "end of utopias," and we don't believe in the frequent separation between literary creation and a nearly pathological sense of discipline associated with the task of writing. I think this is as far as my offer of extraliterary material for generational classification goes. The rest of the story is, perhaps, more literary.

It's become a habit among us to arbitrarily base the archeology of *Crack* on that first, distant time when Jorge Volpi, Eloy Urroz, and I met as undergraduates at a Marist college, thanks to a short-story contest that boasted of authors like Carlos Fuentes or Jorge Ibargüengoitia among its laureates. From that point on, the history of the group is almost archetypal: shared reading workshops, a literary journal as naïve as it was ephemeral, the joint creation of a collective and irreverently anti-rural work titled *Variaciones sobre un tema de Faulkner* (*Variations on a Theme of Faulkner*) — which ten years later earned the Premio Nacional de Cuento — and finally, in 1994, the publication of the collective volume *Tres bosquejos del mal* (*Three Sketches of Evil*). Perhaps that work, now published in Spain, should be considered the foundational and emblematic text of what would eventually become *Crack*.

Along with this six-part harmony of literary youth, those who would eventually become the others members of *Crack* were doing their own thing and doing it well: from a very early age, the ever-melancholy Ricardo Chávez Castañeda became the most awarded author of the Mexican literary scene; Pedro Ángel Palou, a precocious leader in the field of Mexican literary history and anthologies, soon garnered applause for his profound knowledge of the people, ideas, and letters of our country, always filtered through narratives that were as solid as they were disturbing; meanwhile, Vicente Herrasta, who habitually interacted with each one of us as an irrefutable guide to readings and ideas, took his time writing a novel that only recently allowed him to explicitly become part of a group to which he has always implicitly belonged. Then, dispersed, the sextet reunited for years in pleasant but sporadic encounters, establishing connections that ranged from oblique philosophical discussions and gatherings of young writers to collective stonings by critics or in waiting rooms of literary competitions in which our fate wasn't always adverse.

Finally, supported by the enthusiasm of a publisher and mutual friend, Sandro Cohen, we conceived the idea of presenting a collection of several novels on which we had been working separately for a few years and whose purposes, although highly individualized, coincided remarkably well, so much so that at the time we didn't consider it imprudent to design a sort of aesthetic for them, somewhere halfway between a game and the most absolute solemnity, something that would culminate in a literary manifesto.

Mihály Dés asserts quite rightly that the *Crack* Manifesto is as clandestine as was the Communist one at its inception. I think, however, that its fate correlates more closely to Boris Vian's pataphysical imagination. Its only complete version was published in 1996 in an obscure provincial newspaper that disappeared along with its publisher and whose name none of us can manage to remember. One of us has kept a few fragments; another can recite them by heart; and it might be possible to reconstruct a good portion of the document with those segments that were published in the Mexican press the day after it was read. Nevertheless, I'm afraid it would take the prowess of a genuine detective to recover the *Crack* Manifesto in its entirety. To our relief, a sort of mythology about its contents remains: words and concepts attributed to it by those who remember it, but also by those who never read it and claim they did.

In short, there's no reason to get upset about the elusive, almost phantasmagorical, nature of this document. After all, the *Crack* Manifesto has always been just that: fragments, a series of personal attitudes joined together in a document that simply rehashes a single idea — our agreement, shared with many other Latin American authors of the same generation, about the need to break with the more or less recent impoverishment and trivialization of our letters, and at the same time, the recovery of a possible link to the great Latin American literature of the sixties and seventies, the only one that, in our opinion, truly deserves the place in the world that our subcontinent now enjoys in terms of narrative.

Voracious readers every one of us, the signers of that manifesto suddenly decided to utter what was then a poorly kept secret but one that no one dared pronounce with all its letters: three decades after the great explosion of the Latin American novel, the imitators of Fuentes, García Márquez, Cortázar, Borges, and company had led literature down a steep slope where total or totalizing novels were conspicuously absent, as was the spirit of adventure necessary for exploring new thematic, linguistic, and structural territories, ambitious narratives, and especially, that profound respect for the reader that in times past — the time of the Boom — had made him or her a participant in a demanding, and therefore memorable, literature. In short, what was lacking was the thing that confers dignity to any literature. In this context, therefore, *Crack* aimed to make its modest contribution to the recovery of that literary self-esteem that seems to have returned at last.

It's no secret to anyone today that the pronouncement made by *Crack* in those years resulted in its immediate dismissal by Mexican critics. Similarly, the novels that accompanied the proposal and those that came later were not read, while the group itself, deprived of any way to respond through the media, was relegated to an ostracism from which it could not easily emerge. Yet, when the *Crack* reforms were echoed by other authors in other latitudes — authors not necessarily familiar with the Manifesto, although conscious of the disturbing reality of our literature — and when those authors were finally granted the right to read the works we continued to write within the same aesthetic that we had presented at the time, when, in other words, *Crack* was legitimized by the natural currents of recent literary history in which hundreds of young Latin American and Spanish writers have participated as well as by the approval of the giants of the Latin American Boom, who greeted it enthusiastically and without hesitation, Latin American narrative could retrace a path that, it is to be hoped, will be the healthiest one for a literature that aspires to emerge from stagnation.

Beyond the literary prizes, applause, or polemic that *Crack* or similar movements have generated recently, the truth is that the collective consciousness of Latin American narrators today is dominated by a tremendous desire to recover the values of the Boom and of the authors of various generations, from Jorge Luis Borges to Bolaño, including giants of the stature of Rulfo, Sergio Pitol, or Monterroso, who have produced works of merit that separate them from the mainstream of Hollywood props and link Latin American writing to the most noble works of classical and recent literature of all latitudes. It's true that the large majority of these authors, especially the members of the *Crack* group, have partially abandoned certain settings frequently found in the literature of our masters and even in our own earlier work. This distancing from the Latin American context, however, is due more to a necessary broadening of perspectives than to a definitive rejection of the world in which we were born. These days, in geographical and literary terms, the local and immediate can be found everywhere and in all literature. For us, Latin America is as important as Europe, Africa, Oceania, or Asia. Latin American's homeland today is literature itself, and *Crack* aims to inhabit it by establishing close connections, wherever possible, with what any reader with a modicum of critical acuity would consider great literature. It's equally true, on the other hand, that *Crack* is no stranger to the fierce industrial culture in which books find themselves these days, but it is precisely by assuming that reality, as behooves any author who claims to be one, that we attempt to contribute the best works we are capable of writing.

No group can survive without taking upon itself the individuality of those who comprise it. And the only way to achieve this is through a profound respect for both literature and those who read or write it. No doubt, it's not yet the right time or place, nor am I the right person, to determine the literary scope of each one of the *Crack* authors or the novels we have written or will write. The only legitimate claim someone like me can make is that I consider myself privileged to live, work, and write in fortunate company with those for whom literature still can — and must — be a synonym of profound generosity, and above all, of that human quality that, around here, is obvious in its absence.

Translated by Andrea G. Labinger

Jorge Volpi

(b. 1968)

Of Parasites, Mutations, and Plagues: Notes on the Art of the Novel

Jorge Volpi's *In Search of Klingsor* (*En busca de Klingsor*) won the Biblioteca Breve Prize in 1999, an honor previously conferred on Carlos Fuentes, Guillermo Cabrera Infante, and Mario Vargas Llosa. Although Volpi has published nine works of fiction, it is this novel that has situated him among the first rank of Latin American authors.

At the time of the presentation in Madrid, Volpi was interviewed by Joaquín M. Aguirre Romero. In an unusually insightful and informative interchange, Volpi described not only his method of research and his meticulous confirmation of factual material, but also his theoretical approach to this very intellectual "detective" novel.

Aguirre Romero commented that in a certain section of the narrative, Volpi effected a "stylistic change," using "a different form of writing," and added: "I believe there are a variety of important registers that you employ at different moments throughout the novel."

Volpi was pleased by this perception, and he elaborated. "There was an initial stylistic intent and that was for the novel to have the clarity and transparency of a scientific essay, almost from beginning to end. Of course, that could not be sustained all the time, that would have made the telling monotonous. It did seem, however, that at certain moments there was some room for lyricism, the lyricism that is also present in scientific research. Any important scientist speaks of the beauty of theories, perhaps more than the truth of theories. And this is always what one seeks. This clarity and this linearity have always attracted scientific minds. It seemed to me, then, that at certain instants the novel could allow a lyric digression. A very limited few."

"This clarity and this linearity" are similarly evident in Volpi's recent essay on the *Crack* movement: "Of Parasites, Mutations, and Plagues: Notes on the Art of the Novel."

---

1. The Origin of the Novel

Given the speed with which all organic beings tend
to reproduce, the struggle for life is inevitable.
CHARLES DARWIN

In 1859 Charles Darwin published one of the most influential and controversial books of the last few centuries: *The Origin of the Species*. The theories of the British naturalist, together with the insights of Newton and Einstein, have forever changed our perception of the world. According to the philosopher Daniel Dennett, Darwinian evolution is a "dangerous idea" that like a universal acid corrodes everything it touches. It is the only tool devised by a human being that offers a rational explanation for all sorts of phenomena — biological, political, social, or cultural in nature, including our presence on Earth — without resorting to a Creator, or to faith. In short, evolution demonstrates that the complex evolves *naturally* from the simple, that chaos engenders order, and that, in time, this order gives way to projects seemingly as impossible as life or consciousness.

Although Darwin's theory has been extrapolated to numerous fields of knowledge — occasionally with gross simplifications — its application to literature, and particularly the novel, has barely been developed. Leaving aside linguistics and narratology, the theory of evolution has found its place in the world of culture through the efforts of British zoologist Richard Dawkins. In his celebrated study, *The Selfish Gene* (1976), Dawkins suggests a parallel

between the behavior of genes and that of ideas — which he calls "*memes*."*
Like the former, ideas, too, seek to prevail and reproduce, always subject to
the laws of natural selection. While some manage to adapt and survive for
millennia, others just perish naturally.

Dennett has reformulated Darwin's theory in the following manner:
"Give me order and time and I will deliver a project." This seems to fit perfectly all of art, and particularly the novel. The mind of the novelist works as
Nature does: little by little, it orders different ideas until a work emerges.
Like any artifact of the human imagination, the novel is also a product of
evolution, a development that favors the advancement of our species and
one that, owing to its great adaptability, has become one of the essential elements of culture.

2. GENEALOGY OF FICTION

But what the devil is a novel? First, like its blood siblings the short story, the
play, and the film, it is a particular *species* of fiction. For this reason, before we
try to list its characteristics — before putting it on our dissecting table — we
should look at the literary *phylum* in which it is inscribed. What is fiction?
Let us first attempt an instinctive answer: *the opposite of reality*. But let us be
even more precise. As the Argentine novelist Juan José Saer pointed out,
although truth is the opposite of lies, fiction is *not* the opposite of truth.
Despite the fact that it is constructed as an intentional lie, fiction does not
seek to perpetuate deceit but rather to arrive at a different kind of truth,
that of an autonomous and coherent system with its own set of rules. That
is why, ever pragmatic, Anglo-Saxons prefer to say that the opposite of
fiction is *nonfiction*.

Obviating the epistemological disputes that constitute the core of
Western philosophy, it can be stated that fiction is a narration whose links
with past events are very difficult — if not impossible — to establish. The
border between fiction and reality is not clear-cut but tenuous and perme-
able: it depends more on belief than on facts. Fiction comes into existence
when a reader or a writer decides it shall. Thus a text may be considered

---

*Abbreviation of "mimemes," itself derived from *mimesis*.

nonfiction by its author but fiction by the reader, and vice versa. Its character, therefore, seems to depend on the perspective from which it is approached. The texts of both Freud and Marx can be read as novels.

So now let us imagine a genealogy of the novel based on a parody of Nietzsche's ideas. There is no doubt that the tales of early tribes were filled with lies — that is, deformations and falsehoods — yet to the listeners they represented *truth*, since the link between the stories and reality was evident. At some point, one of those early tellers of tales must have realized that he could adorn his stories in obvious ways without losing the attention of his listeners. Thus a tacit understanding was established between the bard and his public: the stories could be false so long as they did not *appear* to be so. Human beings stumbled upon a way to transmit knowledge with an evolutionary success that can be compared only to that of its creators. Unlike truthful accounts, fiction was not subject to strict limits, and could feed off an infinite variety of ideas.

Like Frankenstein's creation, fiction, from that moment, acquired a life of its own, transforming itself into a sort of live organism able to reproduce at incredible speed. After some time, it became strong enough to control the mind of its creators. Its adaptability was so solid — so high its *fitness* quotient, to use a Darwinian term — that it has managed to survive numberless historical misadventures — even outright attempts at extermination, like that Plato proposed in his *Republic*. Perhaps other animals are also capable of lying, but only *Homo sapiens* is able to weave believable lies — from which to derive both pleasure and pain — that contain valuable lessons for the species.

3. NOVELS AND PARASITES

Novels are one of the mutations of fiction. Similar to other species of this *phylum*, such as the short story, epic poetry, films, radio and TV programs, and, lately, some multimedia products, all novels should consist of: a) a story, and b) one or more characters. They should also, c) be in written form, and d) of a certain length.

In evolutionary terms, a novel is a collection of ideas — of *memes* — transmitted from one mind to another through reading. A novel is not, therefore, a book, or signs written on paper. It is also not just the meaning of those signs. A novel is complete only when its ideas take root in the reader's mind. In another sense, novels are *algorithms* — processes that advance blindly from origin to result — a variety of "machines" that, owing to the act of reading, are able to "do things for themselves."

In summary, novels are akin to parasites. Like those organisms, the novel has only one objective: to penetrate the largest possible number of minds and to provoke a series of upheavals — from a simple upset to a chronic illness — with the purpose of reproducing itself through the thoughts, words, opinions, or further writings produced by its victims. The relation between a reader and a novel is similar to the one that emerges at the biological level between two *symbionts*, organisms that mutually exploit each other. In fact, it should not be difficult to measure the efficacy of a novel — its *fitness*. While some narratives become embedded in the mind of numerous readers and reproduce endlessly, others behave like harmless parasites that die shortly after infecting their hosts, such as all those *light* reads that merely provide *entertainment* and are soon forgotten.

4. The Sex Life of Novels

It is evident that novels do not come about through spontaneous generation. Although in theory all novels could be written by a monkey able to pound away endlessly at a typewriter, the possibility that a novel will emerge haphazardly is close to zero. So, when someone decides to write a novel, he has no choice but to visit his "personal library," rummage through the ideas that bubble up in his mind, and create his own personal story. There are always one or two seminal ideas that *motivate* an author to write: those are the *memes* that have reached a higher degree of survivorship than the majority of their competitors, finally turning into a "writer's obsessions."

Once these seminal ideas have taken control of a writer's will, the author becomes their slave and finds himself obliged to develop and multiply them through all sorts of associations. In the end, hundreds of ideas, secondary or tertiary in nature, will have spawned a sort of parasite colony embedded in his mind. When the invasion reaches a critical point, the author embarks upon the task of writing, planning narrative strategies that will allow adaptation to that imaginary environment of his own making. As Dennett explains in *Darwin's Dangerous Idea* (1995), the novelist constructs the work through "minute mechanical transactions between mental states," generating and verifying, eliminating and correcting, and verifying once more. His brain functions in heuristic fashion, selecting the best possible response to each challenge. An author considers the work finished only when convinced that the decisions made at each step of the creative process have been the best possible ones.

5. NOVELISTIC WARS

But just how did the novel, as a species, come about? At least in the west, *Don Quijote de la Mancha* — the first part of which was published in 1605 — is considered "the first modern novel." Needless to say, many earlier books could have claimed that title, but the fact is that in the ecology of the novel, *Don Quijote* has managed to outlast all of its competitors. This example captures fairly well the formidable struggle for survival among novels. As mentioned before, the objective of all novels is that their *memes* spread to the largest possible number of people. That is why it is both immodest and false when someone claims to write only for himself.

Each novel is engaged in a permanent struggle with all others. Since a person — or a society — has limited time to devote to reading, the battle is relentless. However, everything seems to indicate that this struggle is natural and healthy: against all pessimistic and iconoclastic predictions, the novel is not on its way to extinction. To the contrary, its enormous ability to adapt and replicate itself indicates that it has a long life ahead.

6. INFECTIOUS READINGS

Romantics and pragmatists are fond of saying that, as with all art, the novel has no great purpose, whether emanated spontaneously from the spirit — and therefore superior to all other human creations — or whether mere entertainment for the idle. Both points of view are erroneous. The novel is not created gratuitously and — despite the somewhat generalized opinion — it *does* have a purpose, not one but many. The novel is — let me reiterate — a vehicle for the transmission of ideas and emotions recast as stories. Perhaps purists will find heretical the notion that novels have *practical* uses, but this in no way diminishes their greatness. On the contrary, if novels are of such importance to us then it is precisely because in them we think we are seeing what is otherwise invisible, hearing what is otherwise inaudible, perceiving the elusive, understanding the arcane.

The human mind uses two primary strategies to deal with reality: foresight and responsive action. Foresight represents the ability of systems to store information about the past in order to predict the future (and, along the way, to better understand the universe and ourselves). That is precisely what novels do. They are *models*, plans, or maps, whose function consists of transmitting information that empowers us to discern others' motives. Since every human being knows that he/she is alone, and that it is not possible to access others' minds directly, novels allow us to harbor the illusion that we are able to penetrate thoughts beyond our own. The novel, then, becomes a wellspring of information about others; when we enter it — when we read it — we put aside the real world and pretend that this invented reality is ours alone.

The second essential characteristic of complex systems is the aforementioned responsive action. That is, the ability to react to the environment, trying out different responses to challenges at hand and gradually correcting behavior according to the results obtained. In this sense the novel, too, is an ideal tool for responsive action. The reader, instead of having to deal with real-life situations potentially fraught with danger, is transported by the novel into imaginary circumstances he can respond to without risk. The novel is a tool for learning — not unlike video games or flight simulators — an instrument for exploration every bit as valuable as science, philosophy, or the social sciences. Human beings are the only animals who have turned their works — their culture — into their main method of survival, and the novel occupies an essential place in this scheme of things. Different from other disciplines, it is the only medium that allows a person to penetrate the minds of other human beings.

7. Novelistic Games

In order to analyze the workings of a novel, we can apply a mechanism analogous to *inverse engineering*, that is, the procedure one must follow to find out, starting from a finished object, how a precise result has been achieved. It is commonly agreed that the purpose of a novel is not to tell the truth but to fake verisimilitude. That means that the novel must offer a believable model, coherent within itself, that is able to make the reader comfortably accept its rules. If the novel accomplishes this, then the reader makes a kind of pact with it — the so-called fictional pact — agreeing to behave *as if* the stories told in the novel were real.

The relation between the author and the reader of a novel is similar to the one between a hunter and his prey. At the moment of creating the novel, the author devotes himself to predicting the movements of the reader, while the latter constantly seeks to escape the traps laid by the novelist. Contrary to what many theories argue, reading a novel is not a process of dialogue and cohabitation but, rather, an ongoing struggle to the death. Both the author and the reader seek to maximize their advantage, without considering the other. Novelists do *not* write out of generosity or concern for their readers but only for themselves. And the same is true of the reader, who cares little about the fate of the novelist. All that matters to him is getting something out of the reading.

The act of reading a novel closely resembles the scene described by John von Neumann in his famous "prisoner's dilemma." The structure of this model is well known: there are two prisoners (A and B) who are not able to communicate with each other. Several possible scenarios follow. One: if each accuses the other, both will be given a ten-year sentence. Two: if A accuses B, and B keeps quiet, A will be freed and B will serve fifty years in prison. Three: if B accuses A, and A keeps quiet, B will be freed and A will serve fifty years in prison. Four: if neither talks, both will serve five years in prison for not cooperating with the authorities.

In carefully scrutinizing the different possibilities, it is clear that the most beneficial for both would be to "cooperate" with each other (thereby getting five-year sentences), but self-interest, ambition, and mistrust tend to provoke a mutual betrayal (a ten-year sentence) given that neither will dare cooperate out of fear that the other will betray him (thereby getting fifty years in prison). Naturally, the tendency is to betray the other or, to put it in biological terms, cooperation is not a trait that is reinforced by evolution.

Like the prisoners in the example, the author and the reader of a novel are separated by a wall (the novel itself) with no possibility of directly communicating with the other. Nevertheless, they would both profit from *cooperating*: the author by constructing the novel in such a way as to benefit the reader, and the reader by accepting the rules of engagement proposed by the author, so long as they seem convincing. When the author fails to take the reader into account, or when the reader decides to abandon the novel, we have the worst possible scenario, with the loss of benefits to both (money and prestige to the author, time and money to the reader).

Intermediate scenarios are frequent but equally unsatisfactory. If the novelist limits himself to satisfying the reader, it will result in a novel of little artistic worth, driven mainly by market value. The same thing happens when the reader lets himself be fooled by any novel at all (as is the case with most *best sellers*). The ideal situation comes about when the conditions between author and reader are relatively *balanced*. That is, when the author puts as much emphasis on being true to himself as on satisfying the reader, while the reader allows himself to stay in a strange world that is not entirely satisfying to him.

Anyone who undertakes the writing of a novel must try to anticipate the reader's behavior. As a general rule, the novelist does not attempt to cooperate with the reader but, rather, to impose his will upon him at all costs. Although many deny it, deep down novelists are all profoundly *authoritarian*. Their only objective is to trap the reader and enmesh him in their tales, or *memes*. In this sense, their ambition is totalitarian in nature: they plan their worlds in solitude, without the input of potential inhabitants, and they offer texts that are finished when the reader encounters them in a library or bookshop. For the author, then, the reader is an enemy and never a collaborator. It is false that the writer feels, even remotely, that the reader is also the author of the novel, as contemporary literary theory holds.

In another sense, reading a novel implies entering uncharted territory: the reader must overcome obstacles in order to make his way within the text the author has produced. Fortunately, no text is completely closed and the reader may decide to abandon it. Should he stay with it, his behavior will begin to follow the Darwinian rules of adaptation that govern all organisms: learning by trial and error. Along the way, the reader will follow the author's hints and answer the questions that he has left open. When we read a novel, we contribute to its *reproduction*. Or rather, we allow another human being's *memes* to infect us — although during the process we may modify them, thanks to the activation of our own antibodies. In this sense, reading is no different from being impregnated.

8. The Struggle for Existence

Since the publication of the first part of *Don Quijote* in 1605, the novel has gone through a great evolution. Nevertheless, confirming the predictions of entomologists, the emergence of the species "modern novel" was perceived only *a posteriori*. In its own time, Cervantes's masterpiece was not appreciated as such, but seen merely as a new example — in this case a parody — of the novel of chivalry. For obvious reasons this mutation, decisive in terms of the art of the novel, could not be perceived by its contemporaries, who possessed no models with which to compare it (in the same way that other hominids did not distinguish the subtle mutation that gave rise to *Homo sapiens*).

Still, from that moment on, a new branch of the literature tree — and of culture in general — began to sprout, growing and expanding over the next five centuries. Undoubtedly, one of the main reasons for the success of the modern novel as a species is its ability to adapt, reflecting the tastes and obsessions of different periods. Unlike other species, such as the novel of chivalry, Byzantine novels, hagiographies, or epic poems, the modern novel possesses a *form* able to accommodate almost any kind of *memes*. We have here a vehicle ideally suited for survival.

Along the way, a few subspecies of fiction have emerged and quickly died, leaving barely any trace, such as the socialist-realist novel, the indigenous novel, the *Cristera* novel, or the *nouveau roman*, while others have continued to reproduce themselves, such as the detective novel, the *noir* novel, the science-fiction novel, the sentimental novel, and the historical novel. Perhaps it could even be claimed that when a novel is inscribed in what is commonly known as a *genre*, it is putting into play a first-rate adaptive skill, capable of assuring it a legion of avid consumers.

Just as among animals, at times natural selection favors the more adaptable species, not the most valuable. So sometimes the more aesthetically risky novels perish, while novels whose only merit is their enormous ability to reproduce endure. In our own time, in order to survive even a few months, a novel must overcome numerous hurdles. First, it must prevail over other novels. The genre has been so fortunate that today we face a real case of overpopulation. The number of new books is so large that each individual publication has a greatly diminished chance of survival. In order to remain alive, the novel must resort to alternative strategies, such as publicity, reviews, the favor of academics, and that oddest of phenomena known as word of mouth.

Publicity is today the most effective method of reinforcement. Publishers of novels have no choice but to summarize their contents in a few *memes* — a title, a brief description of the plot, the author's life — then do whatever they can to spread them artificially. For weeks on end, those responsible for promoting the sale of books engage in a fierce battle with their competitors in order to get press coverage and thereby enlarge the book's exposure and possibilities of success.

Among the thousands of novels published every year, only a handful cross the critical threshold to reach the zone described in *Catastrophe Theory* and become best sellers. When this happens, the resonance of their *memes* echoes far and wide, multiplying like a plague, regardless of artistic merit. This process has given life to such relevant works as *The Name of the Rose* or *Harry Potter* — the ultimate best seller — as well as to trumpery like *The Da Vinci Code*. The reasons that a novel will have such resounding success are varied — the market is a nonlinear system and therefore unpredictable — which makes it impossible to figure out guarantees for success.

Fortunately, the literary ecosystem is quite vast and sometimes it sprouts small, more or less self-sufficient communities that manage to avoid trends without becoming extinct. These are the microecosystems one finds in academe or among specialized groups of readers that allow for the existence of odd novelistic specimens, assuring their survival for at least a few generations, until some environmental change or haphazard occurrence alters the course of events and attracts the attention they truly deserve. This is what has happened with "cult" novels that are suddenly rediscovered after being ignored in their time, *A Confederacy of Dunces*, by John Kennedy Toole, being a good example.

Literary criticism works in a similar fashion. At bottom, a literary critic is nothing more than a reader who, thanks to the reach of his own prestige, or that of his place of employment, is able to transmit *memes*, his ideas, with a high probability of their being reproduced. When a literary critic praises a novel, the only thing he cares about is defending his own ideas and trying to get as large a number of people as possible to share them. If his prestige (having readers convinced of the value of his opinions) or his reach is sufficiently broad, he can contribute decisively to either the triumph or failure of a novel, to its survival or its extinction. Of course, this argument in no way implies that aesthetic criteria do not exist, or that they are impossible to evaluate. Within a specific aesthetic framework, these parameters can seem more or less clear, and a critic can apply them to justify his judgment, though the frame of reference is still his own opinions. In any case, a bad review is much better than none at all. Whoever attacks a novel can contribute, albeit involuntarily, to its diffusion and the extension of its *memes*. Only indifference is lethal.

9. The *Crack* and Cooperation

Let us now look at a literary society from an evolutionary point of view. Its agents or organisms are represented not only by novelists but also by critics, academics, journalists, cultural officials, juries of literary prizes, and simple readers. In this hostile environment, novelists face numerous obstacles and inevitably are forced to fight among themselves in order to survive — or rather, to guarantee the survival of their *memes*. Like any living creature, novelists are naturally selfish; they seek their own good and never hesitate to crush their rivals in order to achieve it. Given that resources are limited — sales, prestige, prizes — writers wage bloody battles that can last a lifetime.

Unconsciously applying von Neumann's "prisoner's dilemma," novelists think they are taking part in a zero-sum game, that is to say, one in which one's gains always mean someone else's losses. Even though it has not been proven that in the literary milieu the game is always zero-sum, let us for a moment assume that it is. In this case, the options available to a novelist are to cooperate with his colleagues or to attack them at every turn. As happens in any scheme of this type, the best strategy would consist of cooperating — that is, not attacking rivals, and hoping they will reciprocate — but unfortunately, this is the less-frequent response. Novelists are by nature suspicious beings and they do not trust their peers' intentions. Therefore, any kind of cooperation — be it through journals, literary groups, or simple collegiality — is viewed with misgivings.

Nevertheless, only human beings are capable of consciously correcting their natural tendencies in order to eliminate competition and promote cooperation. This is not common, but it has been known to happen. The most natural form of cooperation takes place in literary groups. Although novelists tend toward self-involvement and solitude — characteristics that are highly valued by all — literary associations offer a very advanced strategy for survival, similar to the one obtained in various other human groups. This self-organization should be viewed as a positive sign, since it applies to all complex systems. From this perspective, literary societies are not only part of normal development, but are also beneficial to the literary environment in that they promote the free flow of ideas.

If so many writers and critics remain obsessed with the image of the "solitary creator," it is due to the prevalence of an outdated thought system based in classic economic theory. The literary environment is approached as if it were a linear system of Newtonian origin, where individual "talent" is the only thing that counts. Unfortunately, the literary environment does not develop linearly, so it becomes impossible to predict the relative importance of any one of its members, brilliant though he may be, without taking into account all the other factors involved in the struggle. Like any complex dynamic system, the literary environment is in a constant process of mutation, being changed by unpredictable forces resulting from the interaction of all its diverse elements.

In this light, the literary environment is receptive to George Arthur's so-called theory of increasing benefits, which holds that "He who has most is bound to get more." Contrary to classical predictions, the development of a system is often not egalitarian — that is, gains are not equally distributed — due to accumulation in one place or one moment. If great numbers of computing firms have set up shop in Silicon Valley, or if suddenly there is a blossoming of geniuses in one time period — Pericles's Athens, the Italian

Renaissance, the Golden Age, the Paris of Louis XIV, the Vienna of the Belle Epoque — then it is due to the fact that individual talent is fertilized by the exchange of ideas with other equally talented individuals. No doubt a writer who works alone, with barely any contact with his peers, is able to do brilliant work, but it is far more likely for this "emerging factor" to come about in a favorable environment.

Literary groups enhance creativity because they regulate the natural competition that exists among their members. The emergence of the *Crack* group, for instance, is the result of merging competition with cooperation. Just as Robert Axelrod has demonstrated in *The Evolution of Cooperation* (1994), perhaps a first attempt to solve the prisoner's dilemma leads to betrayal, but when the dilemma occurs often enough — the prisoner's dilemma reiterated — and each of the participants must respond to the other's moves, strategies that combine both cooperation and competition appear to be the most successful response. A tit-for-tat strategy. If one cooperates from the outset and then reacts as his opponent does, be it cooperating or betraying, he will radically improve his possibilities of success.

Surprisingly enough, this strategy has been one of the most successful in the evolutionary field, which might lead us to believe that in life, as in literature, the key to success lies in being correct (beginning with cooperation), kind (reciprocating), tough (reacting to betrayal with betrayal), and clear (making it plain that this is a permanent rather than a random strategy). Although its members were not aware of this at the outset, this has been precisely the strategy of the *Crack* from its beginning. Regrettably, the vast majority of other writers and literary groups have opted for betrayal.

10. CHAOS AND COMPLEXITY

One of the greatest advances registered by science in the last few decades has been the discovery of complex *adaptive* systems. Their origin was observed concurrently by mathematicians, physicists, biologists, cognitive scientists, computer specialists, and meteorologists beginning in the fifties, thanks to the invention of the first computers. Until then, Newtonian analysis was limited to systems in equilibrium, and it was futile to attempt to predict the behavior of systems where three or more agents were interacting with one another. In these systems, in fact, one cannot predict the distur-bances or singularities that will occur in the future allowing for emerging phenomena such as self-organization.

Human thought, the stock market, or the development of the embryo, all behave like complex adaptive systems, the result of interactions among a large number of forces, be they webs of neurons, economic factors, or cells. Novels also belong to this category since the writing of them is not the result of linear processes but of parallel ones; otherwise, it would be impossible to gather their myriad elements into a coherent whole.

It has not often been acknowledged, however, that novels can also reflect this complexity. How? By moving away from the usual linear models. That is, away from *simple* stories that consist of a beginning and an end, that involve only a few distinct and original *memes*, and that are content to chronicle their development in an obvious and reductive manner. When an author knows his characters in advance, knows how they will develop and what ideas will affect their evolution, is even able to predetermine the ending, the result will be a linear novel. On the other hand, if the author limits himself to conceiv-ing the novel as the mental space in which a large number of people interact without being able to predict what the end result of these interactions might be, then that author plots a nonlinear novel, a *complex* novel.

Many writers have structured complex novels or short stories: some clas-sic examples are *War and Peace*, *The Magic Mountain*, and, in Latin America *Three Trapped Tigers*, *Paradiso*, *Terra Nostra*, *The War of the End of the World*, *Hopscotch*, and *One Hundred Years of Solitude*. Unfortunately, these models are becoming progressively rarer in view of the proliferation of *simple* — linear and easily read — stories that continue to sprout like mushrooms.

II. MUTATIONS

The panorama of the novel at the beginning of the twenty-first century does not point to an imminent danger of extinction, as has been predicted by many detractors of the genre. Quite to the contrary, it has rarely enjoyed such a favorable environment, with the number of authors and readers increasing exponentially over the past few decades. This apparent vitality nevertheless hides a more worrisome problem: the low quality of the majority of novels being published. Popular horrors have completely cornered the market, reproducing wildly, and calling into question, if not the survival of the novel as a species, then of its risk-taking varieties.

In its struggle for survival, the "artistic" or "profound" novel — I would prefer to call it simply *the novel*, but there is always the danger of confusing it with imitations — must each day face off against the so-called *genre novels*. Although there is no dearth of examples — Hammett, Chandler, and Highsmith in detective novels; Dick, Lem, Lessing, and Atwood in science fiction; Graves, Yourcenar, Eco, Vargas Llosa, or Mailen in historical novels — little by little, the repetition of the same formulas has generated a rigid system that barely allows for creative freedom. If a writer wants to be successful — by which I mean reach the widest possible readership — he has no option but to include elements of intrigue, history, or fantasy in his tales. As Roberto Bolaño observed, we are witnessing the triumph of the melodramatic narrative: the novel of adventures that unabashedly copies the pattern of serial novellas of the nineteenth century has achieved unparalleled success in our time.

Initially the utilization of such resources by "serious" authors came as a breath of fresh air for the reader faced with the sterile experiments of the sixties and seventies, but their incessant utilization has turned into nothing less than an obligation for writers. Instead of bringing some new aspect to novels, numerous authors — encouraged by their editors — are content to follow tried-and-true patterns, thinking that this will guarantee large printings and instant fame. Unaware that they are following established recipes, hundreds of authors merely tinker — more or less intelligently — with those aesthetic principles. We are not now witnessing the decadence of the novel; instead, we are immersed in the exacerbated mannerisms of detective, noir, and fantasy novels. In a few short years, all such genre novels will seem as subtle and sterile as rococo adornments.

Luckily, despite the plague of genre novels, it is possible to distinguish a mutation that may become a completely new species. I refer to the fusion of the novel and the essay. Even though examples of such hybrid works can be found as early as the eighteenth century — actually all great novels leave ample room for reflection — it was early in the twentieth that the first definitive works in this vein began to appear. Thomas Mann, Robert Musil, and

Hermann Broch led the way, and today a veritable Pleiades of writers from all over the world follow their example, mixing novel and essay in surprising ways. Think, for instance, of Sebald, Marías, Magris, Vil-Matas, Coetzee, or Pitol. All of them have experimented with different varieties of this mutation, at times including lengthy essays within their novels, at times producing narrative essays or concocting truly hybrid specimens.

According to a fashionable theory, complex organisms emerged when a unicellular prokaryote invaded a second prokaryote, giving rise to the first multicellular organism. Perhaps the union of fiction and essay — which is to say, nonfiction — represents the best path for the novel to explore in our time. As we have seen, the central characteristic of the novel is its capacity to transmit *memes* via stories and characters that resemble us all. Essays, on the other hand, have always been vehicles for reflection, although occasionally their aridity or rigor condemned them to a very limited readership. The fusion of the two might well serve to reinforce positive characteristics, conferring more rigor to the novelist's reflections, while the possibility of including stories and fictional characters in the essay would save its ideas from being mere abstractions, turning them into concrete answers to the great issues of our time.

12. The Future of the Novel

As we have seen, the future of the novel seems assured. Despite crises and the recurring prophecies of doomsayers, the publishing industry generates millions of dollars every year. Still, the novel as an art form does seem to be on the verge of extinction. The problem, it is clear, is not centered in its survival as a species but in the potential triumph of more superficial varieties, those plagues or infections that would end up rendering it sterile, turning it into a simple means of entertainment.

If the plague-novel continues to develop as it has of late, devouring everything in its path, it will end by succumbing to its own population explosion and to the lack of readers. Even if this were to occur, however, it seems probable that the art-novel would survive in the margins. Those of us who believe that novels are an indispensable tool for humanity must contribute to their survival. How? By employing the same methods as our adversaries and coming up with an antidote: a community of authors and readers willing to defend complexity at all costs.

The novel is a vehicle for survival, the best way our species has yet found to rescue the memory of the past and to venture into the future. It is an instrument that allows us to reflect deeply about ourselves and the great mysteries of the cosmos. So long as there are novelists and readers willing to preserve this tradition, or rather, to propel it forward and to defend it in the daily war against fans of entertainment novels, it will be possible to keep it alive for centuries to come. The only way to do this is by keeping our guard up: we must continue to read these novels, discuss them, critique them, write endless variations, deformations, adaptations, and recastings of them.

In view of the relentless plague of banal novels that invades us on a daily basis, it is essential to continue to fight for complex novels, those that are not satisfied with simple imitation, that defy conventions, that seek to rise above themselves. Nietzsche stated that the only books worth reading were those written with blood. Similarly, now it is worthwhile only to write novels that open up new vistas and that, perhaps in the future, will give rise to new species or subspecies of fiction. Throughout the centuries, in situations as complicated as this, the art of the novel has served as one of the wellsprings of human knowledge. It is our duty to keep it alive.

ROME, JUNE 2004

Translated by Cristina de la Torre

Permissions

Writers/Works Index

MARGARET SAYERS PEDEN is Professor Emerita of Spanish at the University of Missouri. The author of three books, she has been a recipient of the National Endowment for the Arts Fellowship, the National Endowment for the Humanities Fellowship, and the PEN Book of the Month Club Translation Prize. She has translated over fifty books, including works by Pablo Neruda, Isabel Allende, Mario Vargas Llosa, Juan Rulfo, Claribel Alegría, Carlos Fuentes, Octavio Paz, and Elena Poniatowska. For her work in translations, she has received an Honorary Life Membership from the American Literary Translators Association. She lives in Columbia, Missouri.